FOLLOW THE
SCIENCE?

FOLLOW THE
SCIENCE?

BUT BE WARY WHERE IT LEADS

DAVID GALLOWAY &
ALASTAIR NOBLE

RITCHIE

John Ritchie Publishing

40 Beansburn, Kilmarnock, Scotland

ISBN-13: 978 1 912522 98 9

Typeset by Pete Barnsley (CreativeHoot.com)

Printed by Bell & Bain Ltd., Glasgow

TABLE OF CONTENTS

Foreword...**19**

Preface **23**

Introduction **27**

Science and COVID-19 29

Questions of Existence... 32

Chapter 1 – The Nature of Science............................**39**

The Scientific Method 39

Replication and Reliability................................. 41

Peer Review – a Safety Net 42

Falsifiability.. 43

Scientific Truth... 45

The Politician and the Pharmacologist.............. 47

Deduction, Induction and Abduction 49

What Science Cannot Explain 51

Chapter 2 – The Science of Origins **53**

The Origin of the Universe 53

Cosmology and Chemistry 58

Fine tuning 60

Chapter 3 – The Origin of Life..............................**65**

Abiogenesis...65

Modern Origin of Life Research..............................72

Chapter 4 – Detecting Design **79**

Biological Evolution 79

Adaptation..81

Common Descent 83

Growing Dissent against Neo-Darwinism 85

ENCODE...87

The Fossil Record..89

Design in Biology..92

Molecular Machines and Irreducible Complexity............95

Observing Evolution..98

Information in Biology...100

Mind and Consciousness 103

Morality and Conscience.......................................105

Chapter 5 – Science and Theism **109**

Assessing Worldviews..114

Naturalism and Theism 115

Authors' Postscript...**121**

Index **127**

Glossary **131**

References **139**

DEDICATION

For our wives, Christine and Ruth, who when
they get together collude and agree that our many
deficiencies are almost entirely because we each grew
up as an only child. We are resolutely trying to guide
them in the direction of the research evidence that
provides an alternative view and hope that in the
fullness of time they will follow the science![1]

In all seriousness, we do appreciate their love and
support. We owe them our thanks for sustaining us as
we spent time away from other responsibilities so that
a book project like this could be completed.

ACKNOWLEDGEMENTS

We are delighted to be working with Ritchie Christian Media and would like to record our thanks to Alison Banks, Fraser Munro, Bill Stevely and their colleagues for being so encouraging and for supporting this work. We are grateful to our friend and colleague, Jonathan Hannay, for agreeing to write the *Foreword*. Jonathan has a real depth of experience, forged by many years in both laboratory-based experimental research, as well as maintaining an on-going involvement in academic clinical surgery. We are also grateful to friends and colleagues like Dr Andy Bannister, Prof Mike Behe, Dr Alistair Donald, Evelyn Dunsmore, Dr Antony Latham, Prof John Lennox, David McMahon, Dr Steve Meyer, David Swift, Prof John Walton, and David Williams. We appreciate their constructive criticism and advice. We are especially grateful to Prof Hugo van Woerden who provided us with a detailed critique and we believe that the finished product has been improved significantly as a result of his comments and suggestions.

We alone share the responsibility for any errors or blemishes that remain in the text.

David Galloway and Alastair Noble

ABOUT THE AUTHORS

David Galloway MD DSc FRCS FRCP FACS was a Consultant Surgeon and is Honorary Professor of Surgery in the University of Glasgow. He trained in the UK and the USA as a general surgeon and surgical oncologist. He was elected in 2015 to serve a three-year term as President of the Royal College of Physicians and Surgeons of Glasgow and was honoured with various degrees and Fellowships of numerous international medical and surgical colleges. He lives with his wife Christine in the West of Scotland and has a special interest in engaging and defending a Christian worldview, as well as challenging the default naturalism that has gripped the scientific community. They have two daughters, Lynda and Jenni, and three lively grandchildren.

Alastair Noble BSc PhD studied chemistry and did research at the University of Glasgow. He taught chemistry in secondary schools and was an HM Inspector of Schools in Scotland and Head of Educational Services in South Ayrshire Council. He also served for over a decade as Field Officer for School Leaders Scotland, advising senior staff in secondary schools. Since 2005 he has been a Director of the Centre for Intelligent Design in the UK and has been a life-long member of a Christian church and continues to be in demand as a teacher, pastor, and lecturer. He is married to Ruth and lives in Eaglesham, Scotland.

What others have said about 'Follow the Science?'

"*This book has a straightforward and timely message: the popular view, that scientific discoveries make belief in a creator unnecessary, is not supported by the facts. On the contrary, the more we discover about nature – from the fine-tuning of universal physical constants to the information necessary for life that's encoded in DNA – the more it points to an intelligence behind the cosmos.*"

David Swift, Author of *Evolution Under the Microscope*

"*A rational tour through the exotic forest of ideas and the evidence separating naturalism and theism. The tour guides point out in expert style how to distinguish sound ideological concepts from hollow ones. They skilfully signpost the healthy trail leading to theism.*"

John Walton, Research Professor of Chemistry,
University of St Andrews

"Follow the Science? *is a marvellous little book that concisely explains the strengths and limits of science – as well as the strengths and limits of scientists. It will do much good for high school and university students struggling with extravagant claims about what science knows and how it knows it.*"

Michael J Behe, Professor of Biochemistry, Lehigh University, Pennsylvania, USA. Author of *Darwin's Black Box, The Edge of Evolution*, and *Darwin Devolves*

"*Design in nature is controversial. Whether you agree with it or not, this is an excellent introduction to key concepts which challenge a materialist worldview. Enjoy the debate!*"

Hugo C van Woerden, Former Director of Public Health / Executive Medical Director, Public Health Agency. Visiting Professor, Ulster University. Visiting Professor, University of the Highlands and Islands

"*Science is one of the most marvellous tools human beings have discovered: but can science answer every question? In this short, punchy, and fast-moving book, David Galloway and Alastair Noble—both scientists themselves—show us what science can do, but more importantly what it can't and why. If we want to know where we've come from, where we're going, and what the purpose of everything in between is, we need to discover the God who created science, ourselves, and everything else.*"

Andy Bannister, Director, Solas Centre for Public Christianity. Author of *The Atheist Who Didn't Exist*

"Many today believe that science and religious faith are incompatible. This book gives pause for thought by helpfully setting forth evidence from both physics and biology that the universe points beyond itself to a transcendent cause."

Rev Dr Alistair Donald, Chaplain to Heriot-Watt University, Edinburgh

"A very well-reasoned, logical and scientific account, demonstrating that what appears to have been designed in the natural world, is indeed just that: designed."

Dr Antony Latham, General Practitioner. Author of *The Naked Emperor* and *The Enigma of Consciousness*

FOREWORD

"Good questions are the ones whose answers lead to further questions."

This aphorism was regularly heard from the lips of my boss in the fortnightly laboratory meetings that took place while I was carrying out the research, now decades ago, that would eventually lead to my PhD. I still remember those meetings well. In them, we were called to account for how we had used our time, the agency's grant money, the institution's resources, and the patients' donated tissue samples. All of them, precious. Of all the explanations that we had to give in those meetings, the most fretful was having to outline why we thought some of our experiments hadn't 'worked' ... again ... or yet again as the case often was. We all knew that we had a lot 'riding' on getting results, both in terms of our own security and progress, but also for our boss who had a huge amount of commitment and responsibility within our world-famous institution and an international reputation in this particular field of research. The 'answers' in our experimental results we often saw as 'wrong answers' for the biological story that we thought we were trying to tell with our experiments. Our boss, thankfully, was as wise and patient as he was intimidating and authoritative, for he knew to 'Follow the Science' and let it tell the story of how things really are and be open to the possibility that the story of life and biological processes might be richer and more nuanced than our contemporaneous ideas allowed. Nonetheless, we were well warned against lazy behaviour in the lab and sloppy science!

If truth be told, we scientists often quite like the media stereotype of gallantly-determined individuals putting on the white coat of righteous scientific endeavour, professing an unemotional quest for raw truth wherever it may be found. But we also know that under the white coat the scientist is subject to pressures and beset by weaknesses, shared by humanity the world over. Worries about work visas, job security, being successful, community acceptance, and personal significance, run the risk of shaping the science to tell, or not tell, a full story. In my international travels I've always been interested to speak with scientists who have devout religious convictions, particularly in the monotheistic faiths of Judaism, Islam, and Christianity, as to how they handle points of tension between the story that science is said to be telling them, and where that may challenge what they understand their faith to be teaching. Some, of course, don't want to engage in that topic of conversation, but those who do, don't have the pangs of cognitive dissonance that a scornful sceptic might expect of them, but rather confess to having an enhanced scientific curiosity to ask, 'I wonder why ...' Good questions after all are the ones whose answers lead to further questions.

As you begin this book, I'm sure that some will be wondering if it's going to be 'anti-science'. Perhaps many will have heard preachers lambast the so-called 'proud scientist' with as much scorn in the pulpit as any pop-culture New Atheist on a late night chat show, but, rest assured, this book is not like that. Not at all. I hope that by the end of the book you will be reassured that far from being anti-science it is very much pro-science but in a surprisingly liberating way, encouraging you to demand honest appraisals of the conclusions drawn from scientific data.

Having been asked to write the *Foreword* to this book, it should come as no surprise to you that I can claim to know the authors by their character as well as by their credentials. This should not be seen as friendly flannel in a foreword but it is actually of contemporary significance when it comes to speaking or writing about what is publicly championed about scientific results and what differing conclusions should mean for us.

Character is not without significance in debates, as it is one check on stopping a discussion from degenerating into one-upmanship where the pronouncement made by the individual with the most degrees, or the Nobel prize, prevails unchallenged. Nor should flawed character, for that matter, rule one out of the discussion. Good questions still demand answers no matter who asks them. However, character does still have significance in public debate. Just reflect on the number and seniority of scientists who had to step down from positions of leadership during the time of SARS-CoV-2 response because their behaviour transgressed their very own advice, and weakened the public's confidence in that advice. Character still matters in science and it still requires courage in honesty, persistence, consistency in confession and practice, as well as a willingness to weigh-up other points of view and change: characteristics that I have seen in David and Alastair over many years of observation.

Back in the lab those years ago my boss was keen that we follow the science and report what the results actually were – as uncomfortable with our theories as they might seem at the time. What was always demanded of us was diligence and honesty. Almost any other misdemeanour could be forgiven. For those of us who took the time to think carefully about the scenarios and why our results perhaps didn't fit with our old hypothesis, we invariably came to the conclusion that a new discovery was being made and, along with that realisation, came a new sense of excitement, enthusiasm and joy in what we were about, for the good of others. I trust that you will have the same experience as you read through David and Alastair's thought-provoking book. I commend it to you.

Jonathan A F Hannay BSc MB ChB FRCS(Glasg) PhD.
Consultant General Surgeon and Surgical Oncologist,
Royal Marsden Hospital, London.

PREFACE

As the world has laboured under the effects of a novel coronavirus pandemic, we have been consistently impressed by the confidence invested in 'science' by both policy makers and the public. Having both been immersed in different aspects of the scientific world, we felt that 'following the science' was not quite what it seemed. Science is not a single authoritative entity and scientists have widely divergent views about the same dataset – what it may mean, how to interpret it and how to apply the implications in other areas of life.

This has been particularly obvious when it comes to examining the 'science' in diverse areas such as public health, virology, and economics. To protect the public there are some scientists who call for isolation, social distancing, mask wearing, and locking down of the economy and wider society. Others make interpretations of the same scientific information and suggest a very different approach; questioning the real value of isolating groups within society, questioning the wearing of masks by suggesting that these are known to provide no meaningful microbiological barrier, and pointing to the mental and physical health consequences of instilling fear in society. One of the possible effects is that individuals with non-COVID, acute and chronic diseases like cancer, cardiovascular, and other degenerative diseases suffer ongoing misery and the risk of mortality, as threatening in statistical terms as an aggressive respiratory virus.

Typically, the scientific evidence is not in dispute. The figures are usually agreed. However, the conclusions drawn from those figures by different scientists can be poles apart. So while 'following the science' does appear to be a logical and reasonable policy, especially when we have seen the amazing results of scientific development in every aspect of our daily lives, the problem is that following the science does not necessarily lead everyone in the same direction.

We have been aware of exactly the same phenomenon in other areas where evidence has rightly been trusted but the resulting consensus, on closer inspection, cannot be maintained. That is the principal reason we have written this little book. People are inclined blithely to accept what appears to be settled scientific accord when, in fact, on closer examination, the evidence points in a different direction.

It should not be lost on the reader that an important reason for such different interpretations is hardly related to the actual evidence at all. Rather, the assumptions and pre-conceptions that are sometimes unwittingly used in arriving at a particular inference may be responsible. We will look at how these philosophical hunches can radically alter the effects of following the science, especially in relation to the big questions that we would all love to answer – questions of ultimate existence and reality. Where have we come from and what is the meaning of life? Come, follow the evidence with us, and let us see where it leads ...

The most formidable weapon
against errors of every kind is reason.
I have never used any other, and I trust
I never shall.[2]

Thomas Paine (1737-1809)
British-American philosopher

INTRODUCTION

One of the great achievements of the West over the last few centuries is the development of modern science. From the early pioneers of science in the 16th and 17th centuries to the Nobel prize-winners of today, the work of scientists is universally applauded. The quality of our lives and the development of technologies as a result of scientific discoveries are far beyond anything previous generations could have imagined. From drugs that can beat cancer to smart phones and jet aircraft, the advances of science and technology, even in the last few decades, are breath-taking. Modern science and its many applications are arguably among the greatest achievements of humankind.

It is not surprising, therefore, that science is held in such high regard and the pronouncements of scientists are taken as wholly authoritative. Hence the current phrase, 'follow the science'. When science pronounces on subjects as diverse as the origin of the universe, the evolution of the biosphere, and climate change, it is difficult for anyone to disagree. The 'scientific consensus' on some topics now reigns and is difficult to challenge.

However, this is a strange development because science has often advanced through the work of individuals who were prepared, on the basis of fresh evidence and sometimes facing hostility from their peers, to challenge the accepted view. It is easy to forget that all scientific conclusions are necessarily tentative and subject to modification in the light of further discoveries. It is clear that some scientific conclusions, such as the operation of the law of gravity or the action of antibiotics, are as close to fact as is possible; but some others, like the scientific advice in the COVID-19 pandemic, are less certain and liable to change.

What scientists, and also those of us who are the recipients of their theories, should not do, is accept a scientific position, no matter how ably and publicly expounded, as the last word on the subject. The increasing tendency to malign or cancel dissidents is the very antithesis of the scientific method.

The science relating to many areas of our lives is straightforward and largely uncontroversial. However, there are aspects of our existence which pose formidable questions which never go away, such as:

- Where did the universe come from?

- How did life begin and develop into the biodiversity around us?

- What is the origin of mind and consciousness?

These kinds of questions are so fundamental that they impel us to seek some answers. A number of scientists take the view that science can ultimately answer all the questions posed by our existence; others are more realistic and recognise that science has its limits, and that other disciplines also have insights to offer.

We should recognise, however, that the route from non-being through basic physics and chemistry to biogenesis, advanced life, intelligence, philosophical reflection, and morality is peppered with potholes. The question we attempt to address in this book concerns how good the scientific evidence is in providing an adequate understanding of why reality is the way it is, and why we, as humans, are the way we are.

Science and COVID-19

'Follow the science'. That has been the mantra of 2020. It is as if the 'science' is some kind of monolithic objective resource that would be able to provide clear guidance to policy makers. When the SARS-CoV-2 virus arrived on the scene, initially in the central Chinese city of Wuhan at the end of 2019, it was recognised as a novel coronavirus that was easily transmissible and, for some victims, potentially deadly.

One by one, and at varying speeds, national governments began to anticipate the arrival of the resultant disease (COVID-19) and to take steps to mitigate the effects. Some countries responded quickly and appeared to be very effective in preventing a wave of mortality ripping through their societies. Others were caught out and the response was not integrated or logical or even fast enough. The outcome was that, in just over a year from the recognition of the first cases of SARS-CoV-2 infection, there had been around 100 million confirmed infections and more than 2 million deaths attributed to the pandemic.[3]

> Everything we do before a pandemic will seem alarmist. Everything we do after a pandemic will seem inadequate. This is the dilemma we face, but it should not stop us from doing what we can to prepare. We need to reach out to everyone with words that inform, but not inflame. We need to encourage everyone to prepare, but not panic.[4]
>
> Michael O. Leavitt (b 1951)
> Former Secretary of the US Dept. of Health and Human Services.

Politicians and policy makers were advised by public health experts to take rapid action to restrict population movement and mixing in an attempt to halt viral transmission. The resulting unpopular and disruptive measures called out for some reasonable justification. The regular refrain was that policies were being driven by the science. Senior politicians in many Western countries confidently used 'following the science' as their explanation to a concerned public. Similarly, when things started going awry and the incidence of infection began to climb, they batted away criticisms of their policies and hid behind the same explanation.

However, what was it, exactly, that was being followed? There appeared to be scientific voices appealing for very different policy directions. Face masks or not? Lockdown or not? Take, as an example, the dilemma about sending children back to school after a period of lockdown and social isolation. Is it a good idea or will the mixing of children in wider networks encourage increased transmission and a surge in new cases of infection? On the one hand, there was a contact-tracing study from South Korea[5] which seemed to suggest that transmission was particularly high if the index patient was in the 10-19 age group. On the other hand, reported experience from Iceland indicated that 'even if children do get infected, they are less likely to transmit the disease to others, than adults'.[6] When the scientific data point to opposite conclusions – which science should you follow? At least, the authors of the former study, while expressing concern about its implications, did recognise the need for a time-sensitive epidemiological investigation to guide further public health policy.

It remained the case that in the face of the deluge of data, competing conclusions, and essentially scientific 'noise,' politicians were regularly shoe-horned into making judgment calls. Their official scientific advisers were frequently challenged and contradicted by colleagues who presented an alternative reality. They were sometimes caught out – trying to follow the science. To the casual observer the science appeared conflicted, slippery, and open to widely differing interpretation, thus emphasising the fact that the science was provisional and uncertain. Some scientists from public health and epidemiology backgrounds have acknowledged the extent to which real understanding remains uncertain. Nevertheless, the policy makers had no choice but to carry the can of responsibility – a real no-win scenario! Unfortunately, the associated science has become somewhat politicised.

Interpreting data during a pandemic, when there remains much to learn about the behaviour and characteristics of a newly recognised viral infection, is a particular challenge. So much of the scientific guidance seems to be a matter of contention and the public has been less than impressed that the various questions have been unresolved.

Much of science, however, is more settled and less urgent than the competing theories about controlling COVID-19. Scientists, after all, are supposed to be objective. They ought not to prejudge the conclusions of their investigations. If there was prejudice, any semblance of objectivity would be damaged beyond repair. On the whole, scientists are inclined to resist the idea that their discipline relies on faith and not facts. Perhaps, as an enterprise, it is reliable and trustworthy. You certainly get the impression that some of the bigger issues of cosmology, biology, and psychology are no longer controversial.

Questions of Existence

In the minds of many, science has already done enough to persuade everyone that there are evidence-based, satisfactory answers to such conundrums as the origin of the cosmos, the origin of life, the origin of species, and the origin of consciousness. If we follow that science, as we shall see, we still encounter more than a few anomalies.

The biggest of these difficulties arises from assumptions and assertions that lack a solid evidence base. Clearing these hurdles, as we will discover, does not necessarily lead to the consensus view that constitutes the default position, or the conclusions that we are expected to accept. In this book we will explore this disconnected thinking.

By following the science are we really being asked to accept:

- that the universe has somehow been capable of self-generation?

- that the numerical values that apply to various natural laws and constants just, somehow, came together as a happy accident leading to a habitable planet in a relatively sheltered portion of the solar system where physics and chemistry allow life in our biosphere to thrive?

- that a process of chemical evolution produced the complex macromolecules required to sustain the metabolic and reproductive features of living organisms from pre-existing inanimate matter?

- that the diversity of the living world has resulted from the gradual step by step changes of progressive evolution?

- that a complete understanding of the history of life can be really be deduced from the fossil record?

- that the genetic code, together with additional information-rich systems, has emerged by chance and natural law through some kind of selective pressure?

- that consciousness is a naturally emergent property of brain function and, while it has immaterial qualities, these are illusory?

It is regularly reported that the claims on that list have been answered by following the science. Well, we have been intrigued by these questions and we have also tried to weigh up the evidence. We are far from sure that following the relevant evidence actually supports any of the widely-held conclusions to sustain these claims. We'll look at them together in the sections that follow and we suspect that you may, like us, come to an evidence-based set of conclusions that make sense of the facts without sharing the default interpretation that is usually trotted out.

Interpreting scientific data is not an endeavour uninfluenced by assumptions and presuppositions. The default position taken by some scientists is that, in its grandest sense, science seeks to discover truth about material reality, by appealing to entirely natural or physical mechanisms to explain how things turn out to be the way they are. By the same token, any explanation which suggests that we need to go beyond the purely material or physical realm is ruled out and considered to be non-scientific or pseudo-scientific.

However, there are strong reasons to reject strict naturalism, if for no other reason than that such a view of science cannot itself be scientifically sustained. Those who might claim that naturalistic science is itself scientific fall into the trap of circular reasoning and thus commit a logical fallacy. There is a need to appeal to a principle outside science to provide a basis for science.

In the area of origins, we maintain that some scientists are not neutral, but are driven by a philosophical commitment which rules out the existence of any agency beyond nature. Richard Lewontin, sometime Professor of Biology at Harvard, for example, could hardly be more explicit:

It is not that the methods and institutions of science somehow compel us to accept a material explanation of the phenomenal world, but, on the contrary, that we are forced by our a priori adherence to material causes to create an apparatus of investigation and a set of concepts that produce material explanations, no matter how counter-intuitive, no matter how mystifying to the uninitiated. Moreover, that materialism is absolute, for we cannot allow a divine foot in the door.[7]

At one level you have to admire that degree of honesty, but at another it is quite shocking. What he is saying is that scientific conclusions are not ultimately based on the empirical evidence; they don't 'follow the science' if there is a risk that it might contradict the philosophical assumption of 'materialism' or 'naturalism'.

The problem for the strict materialist scientist is that some data do indeed point to non-material conclusions. We'll come across this in more detail, for example, when we think about the explanations that are used to deal with the origin of the universe. Similarly, we'll see perfectly reasonable indicators of the need for genuine external design to generate the required biological information upon which all life depends.

An additional example that we will also explore has been a source of intrigue for centuries. This is how human consciousness, ideas, thoughts, and memories are related to the activity of brain chemistry. How can those reactions alone convey the rich mental experiences we all take for granted?

For all those reasons, many scientists, philosophers and theologians have been doubtful that a purely naturalistic framework can offer satisfactory solutions to these puzzles. It is much more rational to propose an external, first cause for the universe; a designing agent to write the meaningful genetic and epigenetic information upon which functioning life depends; and a supreme mind that could explain why we are so distinct in the animal kingdom.

Ultimately it comes down to a way of addressing the questions. Do we make a prior and over-riding assumption that matter, energy, space, and time are all that exist, or could there be a real creator and designer of the universe who has left unmistakable clues for us to discover? Did everything in reality just happen by chance and accident, or could there be a guiding influence designing and directing operations?

Which worldview makes for a better end point if we follow the scientific data – a naturalistic philosophy that inevitably entails atheism, and excludes non-material causes, or a theistic view that is open to consider the role of a personal and intentional creator?

Sophisticated members of the contemporary culture have been so thoroughly indoctrinated that they easily lose sight of the fact that evolutionary reductionism defies common sense. A theory that defies common sense can be true, but doubts about the truth should be suppressed only in the face of exceptionally strong evidence.[8]

Thomas Nagel (b 1937)
American philosopher

Chapter 1

THE NATURE OF SCIENCE

Multiple hypotheses should be proposed whenever possible. Proposing alternative explanations that can answer a question is good science. If we operate with a single hypothesis, especially one we favour, we may direct our investigation toward a hunt for evidence in support of this hypothesis.[9]

NA Campbell, JB Reece and LG Mitchell
American textbook authors

The Scientific Method

What is it then that makes science convincing to the experts and the public alike? It is useful to consider some features of the 'scientific method' which all scientists try to apply in their work. This provides an excellent framework and usually works extremely well, but, as is true of all human endeavour, there are traps for the unwary. Real care is required. Scientists need to guard against inappropriate study design; studies need to be set up in such a way that they can really answer the question that is being addressed. Furthermore, it is vital in the conduct of experiments, or the making of observations, that possible confounding variables are avoided. For that reason one of the gold standards in study design in medical research is the randomised controlled trial. A well-designed trial is set up to make sure that there is no possibility that the trial itself may favour one particular outcome. For many years, there was a strong suspicion that smoking was associated with the occurrence of some forms of lung cancer. However, it took years of careful research and analysis to get to the point of being sure that smoking was indeed the cause and not just an association. One must also guard against cherry-picking the results and conveniently omitting to mention important details that might influence a conclusion or take home message.

Even after the data have been collected it is also possible to fall into the trap of misinterpreting results. There is a great temptation to favour the reporting of positive findings; this is certainly true in clinical science where treatment options are being evaluated. It is just not so interesting or exciting if some new technique, treatment or discovery turns out to be a bit of a damp squib. If a conclusion is more likely to grab the headlines, there is a danger that a conflict of interest may determine the way research is presented or reported.

While we have great respect for the integrity of the scientific method, and a huge volume of scientific output is indeed important and reliable, we have also experienced situations where conclusions have not really been supported by the evidence and, sadly, even occasions where scientists have been downright dishonest. Thankfully such examples are uncommon.

Let us make a few observations that relate to the trustworthiness of scientific research.

Replication and Reliability

One of the basic problems with many scientific publications relates to their reliability and trustworthiness. For the most part the replication of results by independent observers is one of the most important ways to generate confidence that scientific experiments can be considered trustworthy and correct. If an observation and resulting conclusions are correct, you would think that other observers would be able to reproduce the results. Disturbingly, that turns out not always to be the case.

In 2013, the *Economist* carried an article *Trouble at the lab*[10] exposing just how frequently attempts to replicate respected scientific research simply fail, thus casting doubt on accepted conclusions. The article reported that 'an American drug company tried to replicate 53 studies that they considered landmarks in the basic science of cancer, often co-operating closely with the original researchers to ensure that their experimental technique matched the one used first time round. According to a piece they wrote last year in *Nature*, a leading scientific journal, they were able to reproduce the original results in just six.'

Sometimes the problems lie with the basic study design or the statistical power or methodology that is used. As the influential, twentieth-century statistician Ronald Fisher said:

> *To consult the statistician after an experiment is finished is often merely to ask him to conduct a post-mortem examination. He can perhaps say what the experiment died of.* [11]

Peer Review – a Safety Net

Scientists typically share their experience, data, and conclusions in the form of a paper submitted for publication to a reputable journal. Part of the due editorial process involves a careful check to ensure that the proposed publication is of high quality and unlikely to have significant errors or fraudulent claims. Papers are usually subjected to independent peer review; a process where subject experts are asked to evaluate a paper prior to its publication.

The notion that errors or inadequacies in scientific articles can be caught in the peer review net is an appealing idea. Unfortunately, sometimes peer review does not live up to expectations either. An attempt was made to assess the effect on the quality of peer reviews when 420 invited reviewers were both blinded to the origin of the paper as well as having their own anonymity removed.[12] The idea was to make sure that bias in the reviewer's mind would be minimised. At the same time they were asked to reveal their identity so that they could not hide behind a wall of secrecy and thus the reviewers would be under greater pressure to be more objective and careful. Neither of these factors had any real effect on the detection of the eight deliberate errors that had been inserted in the papers to be reviewed. However, the fact that was most worrying was that, amongst the 221 reviewers who issued reports, the mean number of mistakes detected was 2 and not a single reviewer managed to catch all the deliberate errors. Not much of a safety net!

The weaknesses of peer review are well known in the scientific community, but the general public has historically often been too inclined to trust published scientific claims. This is particularly the case in relation to the topics explored in this book, where textbooks are inclined leave out the detail of an active debate that is being played out in the academic literature. The need to be concise is important but there may also be a widespread subconscious bias towards naturalistic explanations.

Falsifiability

When a new scientific hypothesis is advanced, one of the key components of its value lies in how testable it is. Karl Popper (1902-1994) was an influential philosopher of science and taught a principle he held to be an essential component of the scientific method. For Popper, testability was synonymous with falsifiability. Although it is not universally accepted, it remains the foundation for the design of the majority of scientific experiments. The idea lies in describing a scientific study or experiment, the outcome of which would contradict the hypothesis being put forward.

Some academics have criticised the proposal that the cosmos and the biosphere have been designed. They argue that such hypotheses are non-scientific on the basis that they may not be falsifiable. Most people are willing to accept that there is apparent design in nature. The naturalist claim is that such design is illusory. We argue in this book that there is good evidence that supports the design hypothesis. Complex biological systems show evidence of embedded information from an intelligent source upon which these systems are utterly dependent. For that idea to be falsifiable one would simply have to provide evidence of an undirected natural process, capable of producing the specified information required to sustain some biological process. The design hypothesis, in common with many others in different scientific disciplines, is therefore, in principle, potentially falsifiable. Evidence of design requiring input from an external source or agent is open to scientific investigation and is not intrinsically 'unscientific'.

Scientific Truth

There are numerous ways in which scientific articles can be misleading. These include:

- a tendency to publish eye-catching results,

- cherry-picking certain details to emphasise a favoured hypothesis,

- sub-set analysis – giving a skewed and limited picture of what might really be going on,

- inappropriate study design or statistical analysis,

- and perhaps even over-interpreting the implications of the reported research.

Prof Sir Mark Walport (Government Chief Scientific Adviser and Head of Government Science and Engineering Profession) was interviewed about this on the BBC Radio 4 Today Programme (broadcast on February 22nd, 2017) and he said: "Fundamentally, science is about discovering the truth about things. It is the most powerful method we have in finding out about the natural world." He may well be correct, but just how good the scientific endeavour really is at providing a truthful understanding of the world is perhaps more open to question than many are inclined to believe.

Writing about the furore created during the COVID-19 outbreak, the authors of a paper in the British Medical Journal bemoaned the fact that so many scientists presented themselves as being certain about controversial aspects of the pandemic. There were those declaring certainty over the efficacy of certain drugs, or the use of face masks. Some were certain that a majority of the population were immune following the first wave, until other contrary evidence was brought forward. There were scientific arguments about viral mutation, infection fatality rates, how to assess immunity, and even about the effects of closing schools.

Their main objective was to recognise the uncertainty that permeates all of these debates. The headline message was clear enough: 'The more certain someone is about COVID-19, the less you should trust them.'[14]

The matter was summarised effectively by Prof Sir David Spiegelhalter of Cambridge University in an interview on the BBC Newsnight programme on 20th November 2020. He said, "I think it must be quite a shock for the general public to see scientists disagreeing so vehemently with each other, because the traditional view of science, which I think is misguided, is that it is a sort of monolithic body of agreed facts."

We all need to be aware of the pitfalls in following the science. There is a real danger, for all the reasons we have explored, that some interpretations of the evidence may be further from the truth than we might be led to suppose.

The Politician and the Pharmacologist

David Nutt was the UK government's Chair of the Advisory Committee on the Misuse of Drugs (1998-2009). His background was in neuro-psychopharmacology, and he was the director of the Psychopharmacology Unit at the University of Bristol from 1988 to 2009. In 2007, Nutt published a controversial study on the harms of drug use[15] and as a result he repeatedly clashed with the views of government ministers. It eventually led to dismissal from his advisory role. He was perceived to be both a government adviser and a campaigner against government policy. There was a media storm in the wake of this sacking and the rhetoric portrayed the government as flying in the face of the scientific evidence.

The media carried numerous interviews with those on both sides of the debate. Most notably, in a BBC Radio 4 Today Programme, the announcer led into the discussion by indicating how objective and trustworthy science really was. This view was not sustained by Professor Lord Robert Winston. His background was in obstetrics and gynaecology and he was known for contributions to tubal microsurgery to help infertile women, as well as developments in in-vitro fertilisation. He was also immersed in basic research on pre-implantation genetic diagnosis to identify defects in human embryos. He rather countered the position of the newsroom anchor and disputed the objectivity of science. "Science", he said, "is not about certainty. Science is about probability. Science is not about absolutes. We scientists give the impression that science is about the truth. It's not! It's about what is most likely."

So, is science as exact as some are inclined to think? Clearly not, but this is what we are asked to follow. It should be clear to all that the world of science is not as crisp and clear cut and accurate as we often expect it to be: it is heavily influenced by the philosophy of its practitioners. Its outcomes are disputed, its reach is limited and, if we follow, we'd better have a good idea about the direction it may take us.

Our ways of learning about
the world are strongly influenced by
the social preconceptions and biased
modes of thinking that each scientist
must apply to any problem. The
stereotype of a fully rational and
objective 'scientific method,' with
individual scientists as logical (and
interchangeable) robots, is
self-serving mythology.[16]

Stephen Jay Gould (1941-2002)
American paleontologist

Deduction, Induction and Abduction

All scientific endeavour aims to arrive at a true understanding
of the natural world. We do therefore need to consider how,
within particular scientific disciplines, reliable conclusions
can be made.

There are essentially three different methods of coming
to conclusions scientifically. These are deductive, inductive,
and abductive reasoning.

To reason by *deduction*, one typically constructs an
argument based on premises that, if true, will inevitably lead
to a firm conclusion – the conclusion is guaranteed. A good
way to understand deductive reasoning is to construct a case

based on syllogisms – the cosmological argument provides one good example:

Premise 1   Everything that begins to exist has a cause.

Premise 2   The universe began to exist.

Conclusion   Therefore, the universe has a cause.

The *conclusion* inevitably follows, if the premises are true.

This example of a deductive argument is a variant of an argument known as the Kalam cosmological argument. It has been extensively explored by philosophers.[17] Notice that the two premises share a common term that in turn is missing from the conclusion. This is the kind of reasoning used in pure mathematics and in the study of logic.

To reason by *induction* is a little different. Based on repeated observation, we may be justified to formulate a hypothesis that provides the basis for a conclusion. If our observations consistently bear out the hypothesis, we can grow in confidence that the conclusion is correct. This is typically the way that experimental science operates. Indeed, the scientific method is set up to explore the most probable conclusions to be made from making observations in controlled settings and testing these by adjusting specific parameters to refine the process. Unlike deductive reasoning, induction might provide a particularly good reason to accept a conclusion, but it can never be as logically solid as a good deductive argument.

Abduction is a little different again, and really comes into its own when repeated observations are not available. This would apply to a scientific investigation of origins, or in disciplines like paleontology, geology, archaeology, evolutionary biology, or forensic science. For example, we cannot re-run the circumstances that led to fossils being laid down in certain rock strata, nor can we reasonably repeat the events leading to evidence being gathered in a crime scene. Similarly, we cannot have access to any real observations about the origin of life or how primitive life forms may have developed. All we can really do in these circumstances is to consider the various possible explanations or hypotheses and try to arrive at the explanation or conclusion that provides the best fit. This method is sometimes called 'inference to the best explanation'. One could argue that this form of reasoning is unlikely to generate the same level of certainty or confidence associated with the other two but it is the only approach available when there is no possibility of revisiting an event in the distant past.

What Science Cannot Explain

There is a difference between things that remain mysterious and perhaps await a scientific explanation, and things that in all likelihood science just doesn't have a chance of explaining – things that are beyond its scope.

Scientific investigation has been incredibly successful and influential. Think of the last century and the dizzying advances in communications, transportation, and medicine. You could be forgiven for thinking that the reach is limitless.

It is quite possible, even likely, that further investigation will provide insight into such questions as why humans spend so much time asleep, or where dreams come from. There are unsolved questions such as how on earth certain species of fish, having been roaming the oceans for many months or even years, somehow find their way back to the river or stream where they hatched, in order to spawn. How do migrating birds navigate? What is energy? What, exactly, is gravity? In medicine and physiology, why do people yawn and why is there such a phenomenon as the placebo effect? In physics – how can subatomic particles in the quantum world appear to be in two distinct places simultaneously? How can dark matter have an effect on light but yet remain so enigmatic? Why is time unidirectional? Thinking in cosmological terms, what, if anything, came before the big bang singularity? All of these questions lie in the realm of things for which further investigation may well provide satisfactory answers.

What about the areas where scientific enquiry cannot reach? One can immediately think about things we can accept quite rationally but which are not scientifically sustained. Science cannot assess the laws of logic or mathematics. Scientific and rational enquiry are dependent upon them, but they are not provable by the scientific method – they are taken as given and accepted as fundamental abstract elements of reality. Science is not capable of addressing questions of morality or beauty. Advances in genetics or nuclear physics may provide the possibility of editing the genome to cure a genetic disease or unravel the mysteries of nuclear energy, but it is not up to the task of establishing the positive or negative ethical implications of the use of such technology. To believe, as some do, that science can provide a full understanding of these areas is not itself a scientifically sustainable view. It is sometimes referred to as *scientism* – a philosophical position – a belief which is itself not scientifically generated.

The fact that there are limits to science is key to the argument that we make in this book. We all accept that there are other ways of coming to rational conclusions and beliefs. We need to incorporate other sources of evidence from past experience or historical data. We can also arrive at rational conclusions by accepting the objectivity of the external world even although such objectivity is itself strictly beyond scientific enquiry. From whatever source it may come, any evidence should be subject to careful and rigorous evaluation.

Certainly science has moved forward. But when science progresses, it often opens vaster mysteries to our gaze. Moreover, science frequently discovers that it must abandon or modify what it once believed. Sometimes it ends by accepting what it has previously scorned.[13]

Loren Eiseley (1907-1977)
American anthropologist

Chapter 2

THE SCIENCE OF ORIGINS

The Cosmos is all that there is or ever was or ever will be.[18]

Carl Sagan (1943-1996), American cosmologist

Philosophically, the notion of a beginning of the present order of Nature is repugnant ... I should like to find a genuine loophole.[19][20]

Sir Arthur Eddington (1882-1944)
British astronomer and mathematician

The Origin of the Universe

How can we even begin to understand the universe? It is immense beyond our imagining. We find ourselves on an amazing planet that may be unique within a solar system on a minor arm of the unfathomably massive Milky Way spiral galaxy.

The earth is around 30,000 light years from the galactic centre. The Milky Way is only one of, perhaps, 2 trillion such galaxies spanning a region of space extending for some 90 billion light years. It is little wonder that people have written of the apparent insignificance of humanity and of our world against such a background. Writing in the *New Yorker* in 1985, John Updike wrote a critical essay in which he said

> *The non-scientist's relation to modern science is basically craven: we look to its discoveries and technology to save us from disease, to give us a faster ride and a softer life, and at the same time we shrink from what it has to tell us of our* **perilous and insignificant place in the cosmos**. *Not that threats to our safety and significance were absent from the pre-scientific world, or that arguments against a God-bestowed human grandeur were lacking before Darwin. But our century's revelations of unthinkable largeness and unimaginable smallness, of abysmal stretches of geological time when we were nothing, of supernumerary galaxies and indeterminate subatomic behaviour, of a kind of mad mathematical violence at the heart of matter have scorched us deeper than we know.*[21] (authors' emphasis)

And yet, our understanding of cosmology has advanced in amazing ways in recent years. For a long time, it had been assumed that the universe was just inexplicable. It had always existed, and the concept of a beginning just did not apply. However, recent scientific and philosophical studies have consistently pointed to the reality that the universe did have a beginning. A universe that has a beginning must, as we have seen, have a cause. Since physical entities cannot be the cause for their own existence there is a case to consider a non-material and vastly intelligent ultimate cause. Here is a summary of a few of the reasons that have led to the conclusion that our universe had a beginning.

One of the earliest parts of the puzzle came in the form of the observed redshift. When a light source is receding rapidly the light waves will appear to be stretched out and shifted towards the red end of the electromagnetic spectrum. This was exactly what Edwin Hubble observed in the 1920s. It appeared that the light from every observable galaxy was red shifted, indicating that the light sources were moving away from earth. The conclusion was immediately clear, and most perplexing for those who, like Arthur Eddington and Albert Einstein, had assumed, even hoped, that the universe was eternal in the past.

Run the system in reverse and the indication is that there had to have been a beginning for all matter and energy in the universe. Indeed, it also points to a beginning of time itself. Einstein's Theory of General Relativity linked time, space, and matter as interdependent and suggested that there had indeed been a beginning – it was most suggestive of some kind of creation event. There are other factors that lend support to this conclusion.

We now appreciate that there is a defined amount of matter and energy in the universe. When that energy changes from one form to another the degree of disorder increases. As time goes by, all the matter and energy within a closed system becomes progressively less well organised. In other words, entropy increases with time – this is sometimes referred to as the Second Law of Thermodynamics.

So, consider this: had the universe been eternal in the past, the entire system would have reached a point of maximum entropy. However, we still have usable energy, and order still exists. Further investigations in cosmology have provided more support for the idea of an expanding universe, which indicates the need for a starting point or a creation event. This includes the rippling heat waves of the cosmic afterglow that have been left by the initial conditions at the beginning of time.

Some cosmologists have been reluctant to accept the conclusion to be drawn from following this evidence. The famous cosmologist, Sir Fred Hoyle, who held to the Steady State Model of the universe, (a model that fitted neatly with his atheistic worldview), was in this category. When he was forced to follow the science, he admitted that he reluctantly had to give up the idea of a past eternal universe. The evidence for a beginning was solid even although he recognised that the origin of the universe could be used as an argument for a creator.[22]

Scientists, like others, sometimes tell deliberate lies because they believe that small lies can serve big truths.[23]

Richard C. Lewontin (b 1929)
American evolutionary biologist

Robert Jastrow (1925-2008) was an award-winning astronomer and planetary physicist, and, although he was an agnostic, he came to the conclusion that the evidence for the beginning of the universe pointed to the reality of a creator. He famously said:

For the scientist who has lived by his faith in the power of reason, the story ends like a bad dream. He has scaled the mountain of ignorance; he is about to conquer the highest peak; as he pulls himself over the final rock, he is greeted by a band of theologians who have been sitting there for centuries. [24]

For a more detailed analysis of this area, William Lane Craig has written an excellent summary of what we know about the origin of the universe from a scientific and philosophical point of view.[25]

Cosmology and Chemistry

Someone has described an eclipse of the sun as 'an experience for all the senses.' One striking observation, which makes total eclipses possible, is that the sun and the moon appear to be the same size in the sky. It is interesting that the sun is approximately 400 times larger than the moon, but also approximately 400 times further away. Someone put this to Prof Brian Cox in a television programme on an eclipse day and he asserted it was merely a coincidence. Really? Well maybe, but the trouble is that there are so many coincidences in cosmology that you begin to wonder if they have been arranged that way.

Paul Davies in his book *The Goldilocks Enigma – Why is the universe just right for life?* writes: 'on the face of it, the universe does look as if it has been designed by an intelligent creator expressly for the purpose of spawning sentient beings' and 'I concede that the universe at least *appears* to be designed with a high level of ingenuity.'[26] What leads him and others to this conclusion is that the forces which govern our universe seem to be set very precisely, or to use the jargon, 'finely-tuned' for life.

We cannot see the forces that govern our universe, but we can observe their effects. The traditional story is that Sir Isaac Newton became intrigued that apples fall downwards from a tree, not upwards, and it led him eventually to postulate a universal force of gravity. This force governs everything from falling apples to orbiting space craft. The value of the force of gravity on Earth is different from its value on the moon, because of its smaller size, and the antics of the spacemen who walked on the moon emphasise how unsuitable that environment would be for us. The value of gravity on Earth, however, appears to be ideally suited for us. Another coincidence?

The chemical bonds which hold different atoms together within molecules, vary widely in strength. This generates substances like silica where the chemical bonds between silicon and oxygen atoms are very strong giving an extremely stable substance, compared with explosive materials like TNT (trinitrotoluene) where the bonds between the nitrogen, hydrogen and oxygen atoms are weaker and the substance is liable, under certain conditions, to explode. Most of the molecules of life are carbon based, and carbon atoms can form reasonably stable bonds within molecules. These can be either relatively simple substances or long chain polymers which are stable enough to be the basis of biochemistry. However, carbon-to-carbon bonds within biomolecules are not so stable that they cannot be broken or modified as required in the processes of life. The various bond strengths in chemical substances could be seen as finely set to give the properties required from extreme stability to smooth change.

Other inter-molecular forces between molecules, such as hydrogen bonds, and in some cases Van der Waals forces, are very much weaker than the bonds within molecules. These forces determine, for example, the melting points and boiling points of substances as they hold the molecules together over a specified range. And they do other strange things.

Liquids normally become heavier as they cool and freeze from the bottom up. Water, however, does a remarkable thing. At 4 degrees Centigrade it begins to expand, become lighter and rises, so that it freezes from the surface down rather than the bottom up. In addition, the pressure of water at increasing depths helps prevent water from freezing. The implications for the preservation of aquatic life are obvious. Yet another coincidence, or, perhaps more likely, finely-tuned molecular and inter-molecular forces?

Fine tuning

In thinking about the universe there is a further range of evidence that ought to be considered. This can be pulled together in the idea that the various laws and constants that describe and govern physical reality need to remain within an exceedingly narrow range or life would not be possible. Stephen Hawking summarised this by saying:

> *The universe and the laws of physics seem to have been specifically designed for us. If any one of about 40 physical qualities had more than slightly different values, life as we know it could not exist: either atoms would not be stable, or they wouldn't combine into molecules, or the stars wouldn't form heavier elements, or the universe would collapse before life could develop, and so on ...*[27]

Bill Bryson has written an entertaining book, 'A *Short History of Nearly Everything*.' [28] Referring to gravity he suggests that 'if it had been a trifle stronger, the universe might have collapsed like a badly erected tent.' Had it been weaker, it would have remained 'forever a dull, scattered void.'

Taken together, all these forces and their associated physical constants make a varied and impressive set of values which appear to be finely tuned to ensure the maintenance of life on Earth. It has been calculated that even tiny variations in these constants and the associated forces they control would make life on earth impossible.

The numerical values that apply to these fundamental forces and constants, such as the charge on the electron, the mass of the proton, and the strength of the force of gravity, may be mysterious, but they are crucially relevant to the structure of the universe that we perceive.

More intriguing still, certain structures, such as solar-type stars, depend for their characteristic features on wildly improbable numerical accidents which combine fundamental constants from distinct branches of physics. And when one goes on to study cosmology – the overall structure and evolution of the universe – incredulity mounts. Recent discoveries about the primeval cosmos oblige us to accept that the expanding universe has been set up in its motion with astonishing precision.[29]

It is hard to escape the conclusion that the forces which govern our universe, from cosmic gravity to atomic and molecular bonds, have been set with a high degree of precision to make our planet just right for life. Sir Fred Hoyle, Professor of Astronomy and Experimental Philosophy at Cambridge, concluded that the precision of the universe implies design. Here is what he said:

Would you not say to yourself, 'some super-calculating intellect must have designed the properties of the carbon atom, otherwise the chance of my finding such an atom through the blind forces of nature would be utterly minuscule. A common-sense interpretation of the facts suggests that a super-intellect has monkeyed with physics, as well as with chemistry and biology, and that there are no blind forces worth speaking about in nature.' The numbers one calculates from the facts seem to me so overwhelming as to put this conclusion almost beyond question.[30]

The existence of 'cosmic fine-tuning' is not by itself a complete argument for design in the universe, but it is highly suggestive of it, and, taken with the other evidence of design in nature, makes a compelling case.

A recent response to the emerging evidence for 'fine tuning of the universe' is the suggestion we might live in one universe within a 'multiverse' with billions of universes, among which ours just happens to have the set of universal forces and constants it does, making it fine tuned for life. However, this proposition is highly speculative and incapable of verification. It also avoids the most obvious explanation of an observable designed universe, which is what all good scientists ought to consider first until there is good reason to reject it.[31]

Some finely-tuned values

Speed of Light: c=299,792,458 m/s
The speed of light in a vacuum

Gravitational Constant: G= 6.67408 × 10^{-11} m^3 kg^{-1} s^{-2}
An empirical physical constant involved in the
calculation of gravitational effects in Sir Isaac Newton's
law of universal gravitation and in Albert Einstein's
general theory of relativity.

Gravitational Coupling Constant: 5.9 x 10^{-39}
The gravitational attraction between a given pair of
elementary particles

Planck's Constant: 6.62607004 x 10^{-34} m^2 kg/s
The quantum of electromagnetic action that relates a
photon's energy to its frequency

Mass of electron: 9.10938356 x 10-31 kg
The electron has a mass that is approximately 1/1836
that of the proton

Mass of proton: 1.6726219 x 10^{-27} kg
This is formed by the various quarks and gluons
which make up the proton. The gluons which mediate
the strong nuclear force binding the proton together
account for 99.8% of the proton's mass.

Fine Tuning of the Physical Constants of the Universe

Parameter	Maximum permissible deviation
Ratio of electrons: protons	$1:10^{37}$
Ratio of electromagnetic force: gravity	$1:10^{40}$
Expansion rate of the universe	$1:10^{55}$
Mass density of the universe	$1:10^{59}$
Cosmological constant	$1:101^{20}$

These numbers represent the maximum deviation from the accepted values, that would either prevent the universe from existing now or be unsuitable for any form of life.

Chapter 3

THE ORIGIN OF LIFE

> One must conclude that, contrary to the established and current wisdom, a scenario describing the genesis of life on earth by chance and natural causes which can be accepted on the basis of fact and not faith has not yet been written.[32]
>
> Hubert P. Yockey (1916-2016)
> Physicist and information theorist

Abiogenesis

Scientific materialism, which excludes as 'unnecessary' any external input from an intelligent mind, requires a credible explanation for the origin of first life.

Although no one was around to make any observations about how life originated, we are not short of speculative suggestions as to how it may have taken place. The notion that seems most prevalent is that, in some way, the first simple life forms were generated as a result of the coming together of the correct ingredients in just the right amounts and under just the right conditions.

There is no such thing as a simple life form. Every single variety of living being is astonishingly complex. To imagine that the first living cell was generated from non-living material and all the necessary structural components, control and transport mechanisms, energy delivery and fuel utilisation apparatus, not to mention the requirement to fend off assault from a potentially hostile environment, seems far-fetched. When you also factor in the small matter of spontaneously enabling the whole business to replicate itself and thus procreate, it can be argued that all the different factors that need to come together at the same time to create life are neither logically plausible nor empirically probable – even from a theoretical point of view. Some of the current theories lack evidence, and run counter to any understanding we have of natural law in the real physical and chemical world.

The most famous early attempt to demonstrate that organic material could be generated from simple inorganic compounds under laboratory conditions was the so-called Miller-Urey experiment carried out in Chicago in 1952 and reported the following year. In essence, the investigators took hydrogen, water, ammonia, and methane as their substrates and in an arrangement assumed to represent the prevailing conditions on the early Earth, they were able to show that basic organic molecules could be produced from simple inorganic precursors. Even the proponents of this idea would be forced to conclude that to consider this in the same category as the actual origin of life is pushing the interpretation of its significance a long way beyond what the evidence will bear!

Stanley Miller and Harold Urey constructed an apparatus with a closed system of glass tubes and flasks. The water was heated to yield water vapour and the resulting 'atmosphere' was influenced by sparks to simulate lightning. On cooling they noted that, having run the experimental conditions for a week, a brown broth resulted and about a tenth of the carbon within the system was now found in the form of organic chemicals, including 13 of the 22 varieties of amino acids which are the essential building blocks of protein. While some of the varieties of the amino acids would not, as it turns out, be usable biologically, others do exist in natural protein. This work almost certainly spawned other ideas as to the components of the early atmosphere and other groups played around with different recipes and were able to concoct circumstances that allowed the elaboration of more complex molecules, including some purine and pyrimidine bases, which are essential components of both RNA (ribonucleic acid) and DNA (deoxy-ribonucleic acid).

Interestingly, Miller himself repeated the experiment in 1983 , this time using an inert mixture of carbon dioxide and nitrogen as a representation of the early atmosphere. On this occasion there were few amino acids in the colourless brew that was produced. Still others have wondered whether amino acids were being formed but were then degraded because of the simultaneous production of nitrites[33]. Maybe so.

There has been much argument about the likely constituents of the ancient atmosphere, but it is not unreasonable to accept that in these contrived but possibly reasonable conditions it was evident that some of the molecules which would turn out to be necessary for life could be produced.

The real challenge here, however, is the next necessary step or steps. Various authors have come forward with ideas as to how such prebiotic molecules could then combine and organise themselves in such a way that some simple life form might conceivably result. This requires, somehow, the elaboration of life from inanimate precursor chemicals. The idea is elevated by a title which may lead one to suspect that there is more evidence here than actually exists – abiogenesis (biological products from non-biological beginnings) – that is the spontaneous generation of life from inanimate material.

In this idea we encounter one of the most profound gaps in our understanding of the origin of life. Let's consider this against the background of a current understanding of the operation of physics and chemistry. Initially it seemed plain enough, indeed it was considered observable. Some life forms seemed to appear out of inanimate material. Before the 17th century it may have been forgivable to believe that life appeared spontaneously from non-living material. Why? Well, people 'observed' such events as aphids arising from the dew which appears on plants, maggots arising from putrid matter, and even mice arising spontaneously in stored grain. The notion of the spontaneous generation of life did appear to be entirely consistent with the observations which people made.

The later discovery of bacterial life forms served only to compound the issue and while macroscopic life obviously required life for its generation – in the microscopic world it was not so clear-cut. It was not until Lorenz Oken (1779-1851) and his student Matthias Schleiden (1804-81) proposed the idea that life was basically cellular,[34] that clarification of this issue was attained. The conclusion that all living organisms were cellular and that all cells arise only from parent cells rapidly followed. Despite that, frustration remained in that, logically, the original form of life must, almost by definition, have come from a non-cellular source. At least that was how the assumptions and arguments were framed.

Clearly there are real problems with the idea of the spontaneous generation of life. While it had been acceptable until about the end of the Middle Ages, the evidence base was really found in decaying material. Serious challenges emerged. For example, the Italian physician and poet Francesco Redi concluded in 1668 that the generation of maggots had more to do with flies than any other mechanism of spontaneous generation from meat that was past its best! He set out some controlled experiments carefully excluding flies from some of the substrate and was able to demonstrate that maggots appeared only in the samples of meat where flies had access and could therefore lay their eggs.[35]

It is interesting to observe how the dogma of the day had an influence on the conclusions that were drawn from the 'scientific' observations. At about the time the Jacobites were marching south, an English churchman, John Needham, was more preoccupied with matters of the origin of life, as opposed to the occupation of the throne. He set out to test whether preparations in which micro-organisms were killed by boiling could themselves give rise to subsequent life forms. Using chicken broth as a substrate he boiled it, isolated it, and after a short interval the micro-organisms he expected made their appearance. Abiogenesis scored again! The sceptics were ready to challenge, however, and modifications to the methodology used by Needham were introduced. An Italian clergyman called Spallanzani repeated the experiment but endeavoured to extract all the air from the system. That was enough to scupper the process of life generation.[36]

By the late 19th century, the legendary French chemist Louis Pasteur rose to a contest set up by the French Academy of Sciences. The task was to attempt to deal definitively with the concept of spontaneous generation of life. He basically developed the ideas used by Needham and Spallanzani, and, using a deceptively simple system, he was able to show not only that spontaneous generation of life did not occur in the protein broth system, but also that there was good evidence of microscopic life forms which were abundant in the air.

So what? Well, perhaps this excerpt from an article by the Nobel laureate George Wald will help to frame the problem:

We tell this story [about Pasteur's disproof of spontaneous generation of life] to beginning students of biology as though it represents a triumph of reason over mysticism. In fact, it is very nearly the opposite. The reasonable view was to believe in spontaneous generation; the only alternative, to believe in a single, primary act of supernatural creation. There is no third position. For this reason, many scientists a century ago chose to regard the belief in spontaneous generation as a 'philosophical necessity.' It is a symptom of the philosophical poverty of our time that this necessity is no longer appreciated. Most modern biologists, having reviewed with satisfaction the downfall of the spontaneous generation hypothesis, yet unwilling to accept the alternative belief in special creation, are left with nothing.[37]

However, scientists can be notoriously difficult to be prised away from their long-held beliefs. Some 25 years after Pasteur's winning experiment, Ernst Haeckel (1834–1919), a flamboyant figure, made significant contributions to various disciplines, but on occasion was not prepared to let the evidence stand in the way of dogma! By the late 1870s he had become an enthusiastic supporter of Darwin's ideas. He famously indicated, against the track of the available evidence, that 'if we do not accept the hypothesis of spontaneous generation, then at this one point in the history of evolution we must have recourse to the miracle of a supernatural creation.'[38]

Many scientists have choked on the idea that their ideas may turn out to be incorrect. Even Charles Darwin expressed concern about how it is possible to hold to an illusion for years. He wrote to his mentor Charles Lyell, the geologist in November 1859 while his book, *On the Origin of*

Species by Means of Natural Selection, or the Preservation of Favoured Races in the Struggle for Life, was being published. He expressed the following and immediately appeared to console himself that, together with colleagues like Lyell, he was unlikely to be wholly wrong:

> *Often, a cold shudder has run through me, and I have asked myself whether I may have not devoted my life to a phantasy.*[39]

How the first life arose was a mystery to Charles Darwin when he published his *Origin*, and it remains a mystery today. In his famous book he wrote about 'organs of extreme perfection and complication' and he was clearly intrigued about the function of the eye as he pondered the curious phenomenon of photosensitivity. However, he did not avoid the even bigger conundrum when he wrote: 'How a nerve comes to be sensitive to light hardly concerns us more than how life itself first originated.'

Modern Origin of Life Research

So, what do modern scientific theories have to say about how life, which evidently has a basis in enormously complex organic chemistry, arose from basic inorganic chemistry? Life from non-life, or abiogenesis? Even if we had all the necessary chemical constituents together with the circumstances that would allow the spontaneous formation of membranes that could enclose those chemicals within a micro-environment, the assembly of functioning molecular machines still remains beyond any currently established mechanism.

For a start, many of the basic chemical components demonstrate chirality. That is, they can exist in different forms. Molecules like amino acids and sugars, where the carbon-based skeleton is asymmetrical, exist in forms that cannot be superimposed on one another. Some are left-handed (levorotatory) and others right-handed (dextrorotatory). Any mixture with naturally formed amino acids, would be most likely to have equal quantities of levo- and dextrorotatory isomers (i.e. racemic mixtures). There is currently no explanation as to how this would change to the set of levorotatory varieties that predominate in life forms today.

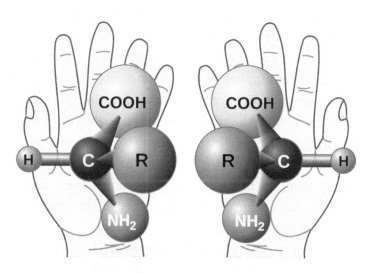

Left and right handed amino acid

It is not difficult to see the problem that might emerge, given that living systems are dependent on chains of amino acids linking together in a particular way to form a folded functional protein or enzyme. If a random collection of left-handed and right-handed building blocks make up the chain, even if the sequence was the same, it would be extremely rare for the resulting polymer to have the same characteristics.

This has been nicely explained in a paper outlining the role of Louis Pasteur in making the initial discovery of chirality by observing the way plane-polarised light was deflected in different solutions.[40] The problem is that chains of amino acids formed from randomly assorted stereoisomers would allow a vast array of options where the configurations would all be different. Left-handed and right-handed variants could be scattered along the chain even if the sequential order was identical. The resulting proteins would in their tertiary (folded) structure be likely to be completely dissimilar. For proteins to work – as receptors or enzymes or transporters or for the huge number of varied functions – their precise folded conformation is critical to that function. If they are folded incorrectly – they are simply inactive; they don't work!

In living systems this problem is overcome in an apparently simple way. Virtually all the amino acids that make up proteins in living things are left-handed and all the sugars, which are vital components of the ubiquitous polysaccharides, are right-handed!

These polysaccharide carbohydrates are important in a dizzying array of metabolic and control mechanisms in living cells. The cell membrane has polysaccharides located across its surface, enabling cell to cell signaling and interaction. These lipid-embedded polysaccharides themselves are the result of enzyme-facilitated manufacture. In a non-living state where saccharides can form, they are random with respect to their handedness. In living systems, they are all homochiral. How this could have happened when, in the natural world these key chemicals exist in different forms (i.e. racemic mixtures) remains a complete mystery.

So, homo-chirality is an essential feature for proteins to operate together in a finely tuned way, or for the overarching integrated control and signaling systems to operate. Furthermore, this arrangement is essential to sustain the metabolic engineering involved in energy delivery, not to mention the need to provide cells with the ability to self-replicate.

What then are the current popular theories that seek to explain the origin of biological chemistry and living cells? Well, there are several favoured ideas. The problem is that neither individually nor in combination do they offer any kind of satisfactory scenario. Alexander Graham Cairns-Smith has proposed that organic compounds aggregated on a scaffold of clay and took on a degree of self-organization. This runs into the sand simply because, even if there is a measure of aggregation, polymerisation, or perhaps even 'organisation', it really fails to offer a persuasive bridge to the massive degree of specified structure and control that would have to simultaneously occur to get life off the ground.

Another suggestion is that certain vital molecules, such as hydrocarbons, were discharged from deep sea hydrothermal vents and that somehow these became concentrated, and further crucial chemical activity was mysteriously catalysed by certain minerals. Such deep ocean floor vents present a very challenging environment for the fragile molecules required for life. High concentrations would require to be present in dense enough concentrations to allow all the required chemicals to be captured in a speculative early proto-cell. Even the turbulence around a hydrothermal vents would not be conducive to the development of high concentrations of a large number of large molecules that easily break up.

What about a more respected and durable option: the RNA world idea? Could it be the case that RNA, which demonstrates a degree of catalytic activity like some proteins, might have been the precursor to DNA and the genetic code? The difficulty with this is the source of the initial RNA whose molecular structure is just as information rich and just as accurately assembled as DNA. It is hard to see how this theory overcomes any of the significant hurdles. There is a well established code, mapping groups of three adjacent bases in RNA to code for specific amino acids. The source of the code, its order and coordination is a prime example of the need for an external designing mind to generate a meaningful rich and sophisticated system from chaos.

The RNA first hypothesis has many additional challenging problems. RNA is unstable and rapidly degrades unless it is found in a protected environment. There is also the need to provide a reliable source of chemical energy to fuel the transcription or reading of the RNA instructions, not to mention the numerous enzymes to regulate and control the activity.

Perhaps metabolic systems, self-constructed from much simpler chemicals, somehow became enclosed in rudimentary cell membranes. Such membranes bear no real similarity to the complex highly-developed cell membranes that we find in nucleated cells. Round micelles can certainly form in water in the presence of large quantities of fatty acids. No plausible explanation has been given as to how these 'cells' would replicate without dispersal of the vital chemicals that they contained. These so-called cells would require to control their internal environment. No credible mechanisms have been advanced to explain how the internal environment could be maintained as distinct from the surroundings. Again there would need to be a source of usable energy to prevent disruption.

Life requires complex cellular nano-systems with machine-like functionality and ability to modify, store, and use energy as required. Not only that but there is an obvious requirement for error correction, repair, dealing with and adjusting for adverse chemical circumstances or biological attack, as well as the over-riding need for controlled and accurate self-replication. You will sometimes read or hear that origin of life researchers are advancing ever closer to an understanding of how life arose by entirely unguided natural processes. This is simply untrue. Goal directed, self-replicating, functional machinery such as we find in living systems has, so far, never been imitated by human invention. Even if it had been, it would demonstrate very clearly that a designing agent or agents were required to explain it.

The farcical way in which origin of life research is characterised in the digital and print media has been pointed out by Dr Jim Tour, an acclaimed organic chemist from Rice University – the ideas just do not stack up.[41] Following these 'scientific' theories doesn't get us very far. No one has developed a plausible set of mechanisms that might explain abiogenesis.

There is one very important point to make here. It is certainly true that no one has come up with a plausible mechanism for the origin of life. However, when the various characteristics of the complex molecules necessary for metabolism, replication and all the exquisite machinery that is necessary for cells to function is defined, one thing is abundantly clear. Unintentional chance-based mechanisms are not up to the task. There is a clear requirement demanding, not only intent, but foresight, code, and integrated systems. The one source, from common and repeated experience, that we know to be capable of producing such characteristics is a designing agent. We'll take this idea further in the next chapter.

Chapter 4

DETECTING DESIGN

I am quite conscious that my speculations run beyond the bounds of true science ... It is a mere rag of an hypothesis with as many flaw[s] and holes as sound parts.[39]

Charles Darwin (1809-1882)
English naturalist and biologist

Biological Evolution

One of the key components of the modern understanding of evolutionary theory involves the gradual progressive change in genetic information, structure, and function and, it is supposed, body plans and species. To follow the science in support of this idea of progressive change requires sequential evidence to tie the story together. There are, however, some problems with the evidence required to support this narrative. The two problems that relate directly to this gradual progression concern, firstly, the fossil record and, secondly, the requirement that functional molecular machinery needs to be fully assembled to work properly. It cannot wait for many generations to gradually come together – it needs to function at all stages of development in order to pass through the filter of natural selection and persist as an advantageous development: this is the difficulty posed by molecular machines that can be classified as irreducibly complex. Michael Behe has argued that some biological systems are so complex that:

Even if someone could envision some long, convoluted gradual route to such complexity, it is not biologically reasonable to suppose random mutation traversed it. The more coherent the system, and the more parts it contains, the more profound the problem becomes.[42]

In addition to these direct problems, there are the parallel conundrums of the origin of first life and indeed the origin of the specified information code carried primarily in DNA but also in a suite of other epigenetic chemical systems.

It is not uncommon for scientists to react with irritation to the suggestion that some of the suggested mechanisms supporting the theory of evolution can be challenged. According to Richard Dawkins, 'Evolution is a fact. Beyond reasonable doubt, beyond serious doubt, beyond sane, informed, intelligent doubt, beyond doubt evolution is a fact ...'[43] His colleague Jerry Coyne, similarly, has not the slightest doubt about its veracity – 'These mysteries about *how* we evolved should not distract us from the indisputable fact that we *did* evolve.'[44] The scientific community certainly regards it in this way and any attempt to question the science of evolution elicits derision or worse. Evolution is also seen as a totemic refutation of any suggestion of intelligence or design beyond nature. This debate is often framed in terms of fact vs. faith and fantasy.

One obvious limitation of evolutionary theory, which is easily overlooked, is that it provides no credible explanation for the emergence of first life. It stands to reason that if we do not know the processes involved in the origin of life, we must remain tentative about its development over time.

Is evolution a fact? It may seem strange to pose that question, but it is a valid one because 'evolution' is not a single proposition and describes several distinct processes. The main elements of evolution can be summarised as:

1. The adaptation of living things to their environment through minor changes over time.
2. The common descent of living things from one or more common ancestors implying the development of complex living things from simple precursors.

These are quite different propositions and the evidence for each varies considerably. Let us consider them in turn.

Adaptation

It is important to remember that what led to Darwin's theory of evolution was his observation on the Galapagos Islands that, over time, certain species of birds appeared to be able to adapt to changes in their environment caused by changes in the climate. In particular, the various shapes of their beaks became important in, for example, foraging for food in very wet or dry conditions. This ability to adapt became the basis of wider speculation about how life emerged and adapted.

We should remember that Darwin had no knowledge of the intricate structure of the living cell, of DNA and the molecular nature of heredity. He could not be expected to have factored these matters into his theory, though subsequent generations of biologists have attempted to do so.

What we do know is that the limited ability of living things to adapt to their environment is uncontroversial. It is known that random mutations in DNA can occasionally produce beneficial effects in organisms, such as the development of antibiotic resistance in bacteria. More common, though, are mutations which degrade part of an organism's DNA with consequential damage which in some cases proves fatal. However, more modern investigation has revealed that organisms have a limited capacity to respond to signals from their environment and make some minor changes to their biochemistry.

Adaptation by random mutation and natural selection is an observable phenomenon and, when that phenomenon is used to describe evolution, then it is essentially a fact. What is crucial to remember, however, is that adaptation through random mutation is, at a molecular level, a destructive process which almost always degrades the organism's DNA[45]

The ratio of negative to positive mutations is so skewed that it is exceedingly difficult to see how such a process can increase the complexity of the DNA of a living thing.

Common Descent

Although scientists differ on the details of adaptation and common descent, these two propositions are clearly linked in that they require, at a molecular level, changes in the genetic information carried within the cell. The accepted position for many years was that the principal mechanisms involved natural selection acting on random mutations.

This is a point at which the philosophy of evolution outruns the evidence. It goes like this:

- science cannot contemplate an external agency which designs and develops living things;

- therefore, such an agency does not exist;

- natural selection acting on random mutation is the only credible naturalistic mechanism;

- therefore, it must be true.

The glaring gaps in the logic of this position are obvious. The evolutionary explanation for complex living things is much more a matter of philosophy than of scientific observation.

Since much of the evidence suggests that random mutations can only degrade genetic information[45] and, although this can occasionally produce a beneficial effect, it does not provide a mechanism for building more complex organisms. The question remains: how can a process that breaks and degrades genetic information be capable of producing increased biological complexity?

More recently, alternative or additional natural mechanisms resulting in genetic changes have been explored. These include gene duplication, horizontal gene transfer and so-called natural genetic engineering. These alternatives may facilitate larger scale change over a shorter time period but there remain challenging problems.

It is evident that Charles Darwin himself was troubled by the absence of what he called 'vast piles of fossiliferous strata' which according to his theory would have 'no doubt somewhere accumulated' before the Silurian (Cambrian) epoch. Stephen C Meyer has explored this in his book *Darwin's Doubt*.[46] The clear conclusion is that neo-Darwinian explanations for the so-called Cambrian explosion (the sudden appearance of numerous species with widely divergent body plans and for which there are no apparent precursors) completely fail to provide an adequate account. It remains an unexplained conundrum.

The fact that a theory so vague, so insufficiently verifiable, and so far from the criteria otherwise applied in 'hard' science has become a dogma can only be explained on sociological grounds.[47]

Ludwig von Bertalanffy (1901-1972), Austrian biologist

Growing Dissent against Neo-Darwinism

The evolutionary synthesis of Darwin's ideas with modern scientific evidence is often called Neo-Darwinism. It is interesting that a small but increasing number of scientists are beginning to dissent from the widely held Neo-Darwinian position.[48] Among them is James Shapiro, a professor of microbiology from the University of Chicago, who writes as follows:

*In the context of earlier ideological debates about evolution, this insistence on randomness and accident is not surprising. It springs from a determination in the 19th and 20th centuries by biologists to reject the role of a supernatural agent in religious accounts of how diverse living organisms originated. While that determination fits with the naturalistic boundaries of science, the continued insistence on the random nature of genetic change by evolutionists should be surprising for one simple reason: empirical studies of the mutational process have inevitably discovered patterns, environmental influences, and specific biological activities at the roots of novel genetic structure and altered DNA sequences. **The perceived need to reject supernatural intervention unfortunately led the pioneers of evolutionary theory to erect an a priori philosophical distinction between the 'blind' processes of hereditary variation and all other adaptive functions.** Over time, conditions inevitably change, and the organisms that can best* *acquire novel inherited functions have the greatest potential to survive. The capacity of living organisms to alter their own heredity is undeniable. Our current ideas about evolution have to incorporate this basic fact of life.*[49] (authors' emphasis)

Shapiro is clearly expressing concern that 'an a priori philosophical distinction' has overridden dispassionate scientific analysis. Clearly, evolution is not all 'fact' but involves a degree of obligatory materialism which corrupts objective scientific analysis.

Intriguingly, the Royal Society, the body that represents scientific endeavour in Britain, held a conference in 2016 to consider 'New Trends in Evolutionary Biology: biological, philosophical and social science perspectives'. Although the conference did not contemplate a design argument, the level of dissatisfaction with contemporary Darwinian theory was evident.

It is important to note that design theorists do not dismiss elements of evolutionary theory, though they generally recognise a limit to its capacity to change organisms. The adaptation of living things to their environment is uncontroversial, although the mechanism for this is disputed. The evidence for common descent and the emergence of complex organisms from simpler precursors is much more controversial, and more speculative than substantive. However, evolution by design remains a position held by several biologists. It can also be argued that common descent could just as easily be achieved by common design.

ENCODE

For many years some biologists have pointed out that the proportion of the human genetic code responsible for protein production is a tiny fraction of the total genome. On the basis of their understanding of an evolutionary model, they expected the human genome to have lots of random mutations which were available for genetic selection as this is a key presupposition of natural selection. They hypothesised, rather prematurely as it turns out, that the remaining DNA sequences were largely chaotic refuse left over from aeons of evolutionary change – so called 'junk DNA.'

Given that we are still at a relatively early stage in unravelling the functional mysteries of the DNA code and exactly how it works, it surely must have occurred to them that there may be more to this large volume of material, with an as yet undetermined function, than genetic flotsam and jetsam. The thinking was that in amongst the inactive DNA sequences, any mutations would not influence function and would therefore not be selectable but would simply accumulate steadily with time. This 'junk' was considered to be a useless by-product from previous mutations in now inactive genes, pseudogenes, gene fragments, and other discarded sequences. When the Human Genome Project Director Francis Collins wrote his book *The Language of God* in 2006, he believed that this genetic detritus provided supporting evidence for the Darwinian story of gradual mutation and natural selection.[50] Similarly, other authors wrote of our genome being 'well populated graveyards of dead genes.'[44]

When the ENCODE Project Consortium published their initial findings in Nature in September 2012, the notion that the bulk of the genome was inactive was blown away.[51] They sought to define all the functional elements encoded in the human genome. As increasingly powerful DNA sequencing technology has become available, so more extensive and precise analyses have become possible. Segments encoding an identifiable product or displaying particular biochemical activity like protein or chromatin binding were examined. They studied multiple cell types and found genetically driven influence to enhance or constrain certain activities. Rather than being inactive, they outlined biochemical activity and function for 80.4% of the human genome. This applied particularly to areas outside the previously well-studied protein coding regions.

It has become clear that many of these regions are involved in the regulation of gene expression. The human body is composed of trillions of cells, with over 200 different cell types. At different stages of the development of an organism, some activity may be important in the embryo but must be down-regulated or turned off in the adult. There is also a regulatory role required to control protein production. Some of the DNA is not even transcribed into RNA, but is still biochemically active.

Subsequent publications from the ENCODE group have followed and have demonstrated many more examples of switches and control mechanisms and areas thought to be silent that are actually, according to the senior ENCODE research scientist Ewan Birney, 'teeming with things going on; we still really don't understand that.'[52]

Removing the force of the junk DNA argument has caused one of the significant pillars of gradual, slow evolutionary Darwinian thinking to crumble. That argument can no longer be sustained to support such a narrative. Birney further commented that 'it's very hard to get over the density of information' in the genome.[52] Not only that but as we will go on to outline – the source of genuine, sophisticated, meaningful, and detailed information in the genome is significant evidence for the need of genuine design in genetics and epigenetics.

The Fossil Record

The widely accepted popular view of the gradual change from one life form and one species to another purports to take support from the fossil record. This is assumed to demonstrate various life forms slowly and progressively evolving one to another. In fact, the fossil record is replete with discontinuities. Richard Dawkins in a famous debate at the Oxford Union indicated: "Of course there are gaps, that is exactly what you would expect!" The idea is that the many gaps are simply artefacts because, by its nature, the record is incomplete. According to Darwin's most vocal modern disciple, "there is not the slightest shadow of a doubt in the mind of anybody who has seriously considered the matter that the theory of evolution is true."[53] The way he handles concerns about gaps in the fossil record is interesting. In mocking terms, he addressed the claim that 'the fossil record is full of gaps' and retorted:

Well of course the fossil record is full of gaps! What on earth do you expect? When you do human history, you don't expect to find a complete narrative record of every single thing that happened every single day … you piece it together. If there were no gaps, you'd think there were something pretty funny going on.

He goes on to claim that:

The fossil record, in spite of the gaps, provides overwhelmingly strong evidence for evolution.[27]

It is certainly possible to conclude that the fossil record consists of an orderly sequence in which the major groups of organisms appear successively in higher and more recent strata. It has also to be said that an inconsistency in the fossil record is not necessarily evidence against evolution. There are some considerations that need to be brought to the fore.

One might reasonably expect there to be better evidence of a finely graduated chain of variants. The evolutionary palaeontologist, Stephen Jay Gould, conceded that:

The absence of fossil evidence for intermediary stages between major transitions in organic design, indeed our inability, even in our imagination, to construct functional intermediates in many cases, has been a persistent and nagging problem for gradualistic accounts of evolution.[54]

His colleague Niles Eldredge commented:

The record jumps, and all the evidence shows that the record is real: the gaps we see reflect real events in life's history – not the artefact of a poor fossil record. [55]

The famous palaeontologist, David M. Raup (1933-2015), who did much of his work at the Field Museum of Chicago, addressed this issue head on and, allowing for the 120 or so years since Darwin published, wrote:

'*We now have a quarter of a million fossil species, but the situation hasn't changed much. The record of evolution is still surprisingly jerky and, ironically, we have even fewer examples of evolutionary transitions than we had in Darwin's time. By this I mean that some of the classic cases of Darwinian change in the fossil record, such as the evolution of the horse in North America, have had to be discarded or modified as a result of more detailed information – what appeared to be a nice simple progression when relatively few data were available now appear to be much more complex and much less gradualistic. So Darwin's problem has not been alleviated in the last 120 years and we still have a record which does show change but one that can hardly be looked upon as the most reasonable consequence of natural selection.*' [56]

An additional concern relates to the assumptions used in the very approach to interpreting the fossil evidence. While methods such as radiometric dating can be used to provide an assessment of the age of a particular rock layer, the occurrence of certain fossils within a sediment are not infrequently used to provide an index of the geological age of the layer itself. The fossils are thus used as evidence for dating the rock. If, in turn, it is assumed that life evolved from simple to complex forms over long periods of time, as might be derived from an understanding of geological layers laid down successively, we risk committing the circular fallacy of allowing the rocks to date the fossils or the fossils to date the rocks! So which is it to be? If we allow both, it commits the logical fallacy of arguing in a circle. We assume the conclusion to build the case for the conclusion!

Design in Biology

It is strange that to mention 'design' in biology is virtually to commit an academic offence. The general view is that Darwin makes design unnecessary, and this despite the observations of leading scientists like Dawkins[57] and Davies[26] that nature gives 'the appearance of design'. Many feel intuitively that the wonders of nature could not have arisen by chance and that they show evidence of a designing intelligence. However, to think that way is not, apparently, to follow the science.

Prof Steve Fuller of Warwick University, England, has commented on this as follows:

*… from cosmology to biology, it is becoming increasingly clear that science's failure to explain matters at the most fundamental level is at least in part due to **an institutional prohibition on intelligent design** as one of the explanatory options.*[58] (authors' emphasis)

He goes on to point out that this prohibition goes by the name of 'methodological naturalism', but it could equally be 'methodological atheism'. This is a classic case of philosophy overtaking scientific evidence and is certainly not an example of 'following the science'.

So, it is useful to stand back a little and consider how we recognise design. We doubt that most of us have ever given much thought to that. The recognition of design in the multitude of objects around us, from motor cars to garden sheds, is so natural that we seldom think about it. What then distinguishes something as being designed?

One answer is that design involves the purposeful arrangement of parts. In other words, there is a level of organisation that could not happen naturally and has required the intervention of an intelligent agent. As someone has pointed out, a Boeing 747 does not arise from an explosion in a junk yard any more than a garden shed arises from a storm in a forest.[59]

An interesting exercise is to invite suggestions as to what in a room might not be designed. When put on one occasion to a class of senior school pupils by one of the authors, the answers, after considerable thought, were the arrangement of the contents of a waste bin or the ashes from a fire. Both are good examples, although the objects in a waste bin are clearly individually designed, but their random disposal is not. If you wanted to be pedantic, you could argue that the molecular and atomic structure of ashes, if we could see it, are highly complex, but a pile of grey ashes in a fireplace is clearly not designed. These examples are, nonetheless, legitimate and illustrate how few objects in our daily lives are not designed by someone.

Another example of deliberate design might be found on a walk on the beach. There will be plenty of examples of regular ripples in the sand because of the movement of the tides. Although these are impressive, we recognise that they come from the operation of natural laws governing the motion of sea water and not directly designed. If, however, we find a tracing on the sand with an arrow through a heart and the words 'John loves Mary', we would not think twice about whether it was designed. It was obviously the work of an amorous suitor!

So, how do we define design? The purposeful arrangement of parts which are unlikely to have self-assembled is one answer. Another answer is that design involves complexity which has been specified elsewhere. So, if we look at a house, we know that its construction started in an architect's mind and that the plans for it could be found, if necessary, in his firm's office. All the sophisticated equipment we use daily from electric kettles to fast cars are specified somewhere in designers' charts or computer software. And the ideas for them arose at first in someone's mind.

A working definition of design, therefore, is that it involves 'specified complexity'. Note that some complex things, like the pattern of the clouds or the distribution of trees in a wild forest, are complex, but they have not been directly specified and are, therefore, not designed in an immediate sense. Of course, the complexity of clouds and trees point to a deeper level of order in the universe. But most everyday objects have both complexity and specificity, pointing to a design plan in a designer's mind.

Molecular Machines and Irreducible Complexity

So how does all this relate to complex biological structures? One biologist who has devoted a considerable amount of thought to this is Prof Michael Behe, a biochemist at Lehigh University, Pennsylvania. He has written several books on the subject. One of the first biological mechanisms that caught his attention was the bacterial flagellum. Up to that point, as a biochemist, he never had any reason to question Darwinian mechanisms.[60]

Some bacteria have one or more tails or flagella which enable them to swim through fluid. When Behe first saw a bacterial flagellum under an electron microscope, which can provide a magnification of up to 50 million times, he saw its 30 or so components, some structural as well as some moving parts, which are made of protein. He immediately recognised the similarity to an outboard motor. Further investigation has revealed that the flagellum can rotate at up to 100,000 revolutions per minute and change direction on a quarter of a turn. Also, if any one of its 30 or so moving parts were disabled, the mechanism failed to work. Behe began to wonder how such a sophisticated system could possibly have evolved over time. Unless all the parts were present, it would not work, and intermediates with only some of the parts would not be functional and, therefore, would be rejected by evolutionary processes.

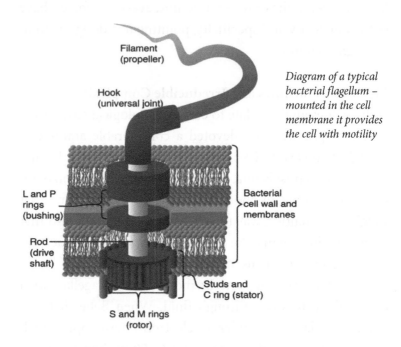

Diagram of a typical bacterial flagellum – mounted in the cell membrane it provides the cell with motility

Behe coined the phrase 'irreducible complexity' for sophisticated biological systems like the flagellum. It means that all the parts are necessary before function is achieved. If any components were lost or damaged the overall function would fail. He increasingly came to see that structures like the flagellum defied any gradual evolutionary development.

Each and every gradual modification would need to demonstrate some function offering a survival advantage and, therefore, be selectable. Since the machine does not function properly until it is all fully assembled, a gradual evolutionary mechanism simply cannot explain its development.

And not only is there the sheer complexity of the flagellum, but the information which specifies it lies in the bacterial DNA. Subsequent work has indicated how the various parts of the flagellum are transported to, and assembled in, their position in the structure.[61] This is unquestionably an example of 'irreducible complexity' which is specified in the genetic code. Darwinian explanations involving random construction, natural selection, and gradual change seem highly improbable as explanations of the origin and development of bacterial flagella, cilia, or a range of other components built from a combination of structural and motor proteins such as myosins, dyneins, and kinesins.

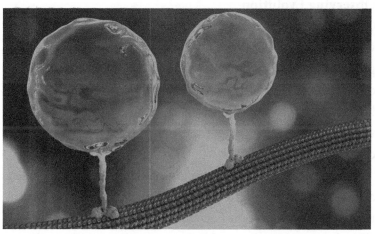

Kinesin motor proteins 'walking' along a microtubule

Furthermore, living things teem with irreducibly complex mechanisms such as, at the molecular level, the Krebs cycle in intermediary metabolism, blood-clotting in mammals, nucleic acid replication, enzyme production, and systems with sophisticated feedback signalling and control. It is just as persuasive at the level of tissues, organs, and overall body plans. In humans (and other mammals) consider, for example, the vital co-ordinated switching in oxygen delivery that takes place at birth from a placental blood supply to newly functioning lungs. Or think about the incredible systematic feedback and control of blood pressure and heart rate, or the exquisite detail and sophistication of the endocrine system. The irreducible complexity of many biological systems presents a massive challenge to accepted Darwinian theories of origin and development. It rather points to deliberate design.

Observing Evolution

One of the difficulties in biology is to devise experiments which can validate what is claimed for evolutionary processes. The difficulty is two-fold: firstly, the number of organisms and intermediates whose behaviour one would have to observe is enormous; and, secondly, evolution takes such a prohibitively long time that its progress cannot be directly observed.

However, the American biologist Richard Lenski devised a way of getting close to real evolutionary timescales. Using the common bacterium *E. coli*, he set up a series of cultures. This fast-growing bug, which can produce about a dozen generations in 24 hours, provided a means of studying changes over many generations.

Lenski's experiment has now run for a quarter of a century. By withdrawing small samples at frequent intervals and creating new cultures, he has studied, to date, the bacteria over more than 50,000 generations – a number that is comparable to over a million years for a large animal species. Clearly this is a highly credible experiment for assessing the extent of evolutionary changes.

So, what have the Lenski experiments shown? Well, for a start, the bacterial growth rate and the size of the microbes increased significantly. It was also noted, however, that the bacterial ability to metabolise some nutrients like the sugar ribose was lost. With the more recent availability of DNA sequencing, the experimenters were able to observe changes in the bacterial genome and found that several areas of its DNA had been degraded and had reduced function. However, although there had been some significant changes in the behaviour of the bacterium, the *E. coli* was still recognisable as the same species but with some deterioration in its metabolic activity. Although Lenski may view his experiments as evidence for some aspects of evolution, it can be argued that the lack of major shifts in the DNA over many thousands of generations suggests that *E. coli* are relatively stable over time. This challenges aspects of the overriding evolutionary paradigm, which might have predicted greater change over that number of generations.

Michael Behe, describing Lenski's work in his recent book, *Darwin Devolves*, comments:

The bottom line is this. After fifty thousand generations of the most detailed, definitive evolution experiment ever conducted, after so much improvement of the growth rate that descendent cells leave revived ancestors in the dust, after relentless mutation and selection, it's very likely that all of the identified beneficial mutations worked by degrading or outright breaking the respective ancestor genes. And the havoc wreaked by random mutation had been frozen in place by natural selection.[45]

In terms of current evolutionary theory, it appears to have failed to provide evidence to support large-scale change in the DNA.

Information in Biology

One of the great chemical discoveries of the modern world was the elucidation of the double helical molecular structure of DNA by Crick and Watson in 1953. For years, the mechanism of heredity by which living things passed their characteristics to the next generation remained a mystery. Now it is apparent that this lies in the arrangement of the chemical units within the structure of the DNA molecule.

It is interesting that the phrase 'genetic code' emerged from Crick and Watson's work, implying that the structure of the DNA carries instructions and information that determines the biological features of the organism involved. Someone has commented that in unravelling the mystery of the molecular structure of DNA, Crick and Watson solved one problem but created another. If DNA carries real genetic information, what is the source of that information?

Few of us will become software programmers, but most of us do understand that computers run on the sophisticated digital code that has been embedded in them. These programmes are complex arrangements of the 1s and 0s which are used as computer code. We would never accept that computer programmes could arise randomly or by accident and we realise that any random interference with them would degrade the software considerably.

Few people know more about computers than Bill Gates, co-founder of the Microsoft Corporation. In his book *The Road Ahead* he has written: 'DNA is like a computer program but far, far more advanced than any software ever created.'[62] Now, if Bill Gates employs the best minds in the software world to generate Microsoft's programmes, what conclusion can we draw about the programming of DNA?

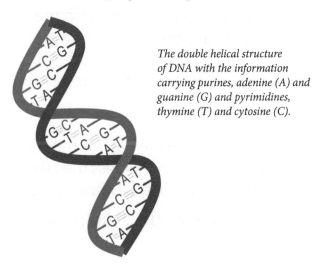

The double helical structure of DNA with the information carrying purines, adenine (A) and guanine (G) and pyrimidines, thymine (T) and cytosine (C).

Increasingly, we are beginning to realise that the foundation of biology is information, coded into the DNA of all living things. Information, wherever we find it, is a real phenomenon, immaterial certainly, and in the case of computers, carried in the sequences coded into the software. As computer software is ultimately traceable to the mind of the programmer, it is reasonable to infer that the genetic information carried in DNA reflects the activity of mind. That is why some scientists see, in the information content of DNA, clear evidence of a supreme intelligence. The alternative proposition that it arose in the primeval earth, somehow, by chance or by accident, is much more a philosophical necessity than a scientific conclusion.

There is no known law of nature, no known process and no known sequence of events which can cause information to originate by itself in matter.[63]

Werner Gitt (b 1937), German engineer

Ultimately, the Darwinian theory of evolution is no more nor less than the great cosmogenic myth of the twentieth century.[64]

Michael Denton (b 1943), Australian biochemist

Mind and Consciousness

Sometimes, it is the most obvious things that escape our attention. When we consider just about anything we choose to do, behind it lies our mind, which directs our actions. Even to contemplate a course of action we use our minds to think it through, and sometimes our reason dissuades us from taking a course which might prove damaging to us. We are obviously conscious and thoughtful beings, and we would normally be offended if someone suggested to us that we acted irrationally. So where do the immaterial realities of mind, consciousness, and rationality come from?

These matters pose serious questions for methodological naturalism, which is obliged, for philosophical reasons, to conclude that mind and consciousness are somehow the product of chance and evolution. If that thesis is true, then how does rational thought arise? And how can we trust anything that we think or propose if the origin of our reason is accidental and random? We cannot, obviously, and it can be argued that such a position makes the practice of science, or any intellectual activity for that matter, devoid of a solid logical foundation for assuming that true answers exist and are discoverable.

In *Darwin Devolves*,[45] Michael Behe summarises the problem thus:

Failure to recognise the conspicuous explanation for life is due wholly to the explicit denial by evolutionary biology and other contemporary scholarly disciplines of the necessary foundation for any kind of knowledge – that mind is real.

In his remarkable 2012 book, *Mind and Cosmos*, with the astonishing sub-title *Why the Materialist Neo-Darwinian Conception of Nature is Almost Certainly False*, Thomas Nagel, Professor of Philosophy at New York University, writes:

My guiding conviction is that mind is not just an afterthought or an accident or an add-on, but a basic aspect of nature ... Science is driven by the assumption that the world is intelligible.

and later adds:

Consciousness is the most conspicuous obstacle to a comprehensive naturalism that relies only on the resources of physical science.[65]

It is intriguing that Nagel is an atheist, yet he recognises that mind is a prerequisite to explain the origin and functioning of the natural world.

In his book, *Signature in the Cell*, Dr Stephen Meyer, a geologist and philosopher of science, deals with these issues in a remarkable paragraph, in which he quotes historian of science, Peter Hodgson.

The assumption that a rational mind had designed the universe gave rise to two ideas – intelligibility and contingency – which, in turn, provided a powerful impetus to study nature and feel confident that such study would yield understanding. As the Oxford physicist and historian of science Peter Hodgson observes: 'According to Judeo-Christian beliefs, the world is the free creation of God from nothing. The structure of the world cannot therefore be deduced from first principles; we have to look at it, to make observations and experiments to find out how God made it. This reinforces the Aristotelian principle that all knowledge comes through the senses but requires that it be situated within a wider set of beliefs concerning the nature of the world that is implicit in the doctrine of creation.' [66]

It seems, therefore, that it is the pre-existence of mind before matter which makes the scientific study of the world valid. If that is not the case, our minds cannot provide a reliable basis for any kind of logical investigation.

Morality and Conscience

Humans appear to be unique within the living world. There is no good evidence that other members of the animal kingdom have the ability to think philosophically and reason for themselves. Nor is there any suggestion that other life forms process the ideas of right and wrong, or guilt and innocence. Furthermore, an important distinctive of humanity is the amazing capacity for artistic and scientific creativity as displayed in music, the visual and dramatic arts, and the role of problem solving and invention. Perhaps the most compelling and valuable human distinctive is the capacity to form relationships and experience love as more than simply some kind of driven endocrine activity. Beyond this lies the sense of appreciation for truth and an ability to think and behave with a view to making moral choices. So where does this moral realm come from, especially given that it is a category that just does not apply to other mammals or life forms?

A huge amount of ink has been spilled in speculations about the evolutionary and social hypotheses advanced to explain moral behaviour in humans. A common assumption is that these features are simply adaptive – cohesive groups, where interdependence is an important function, which can survive rather better if some kind of moral code applies and is transmitted through the generations.[67] The argument runs that moral conduct emerges as a means of establishing social norms, managing conflict, and helping to maintain and control identity and group solidarity.

We recognise that organisms have genes that code for an ability to survive and reproduce; but could it be the case that there is a biochemical basis, perhaps through the agency of certain hormones, that result in an instinctive desire to care for the weak and the young? It is certainly the case that a range of ideas and theories abound in this area – more reliant on assumption and assertion than in anything approaching scientific fact.

The atheist philosopher Peter Singer, the primary contributor to the *Encyclopaedia Britannica* section on the Origin of Ethics,[68] gives an historical account of the production of the first ethical codes. His suggestion is that an appreciation of morality emerged when humans began to reflect upon the best way to live. He hints also at the perfectly valid reasons for attributing a moral law to a divine source – a moral lawgiver. Indeed, while not specifically an argument of science, (morality, aesthetics, and truth are all categories that are not directly open to scientific enquiry) it is nevertheless the case that an important deductive argument for the reality of God's existence is known as the moral argument. It can be expressed like this:

- Premise 1: If God does not exist, objective moral values and duties do not exist.

- Premise 2: Objective moral values and duties do exist.

- Conclusion: Therefore, God exists.

Taken together with the scientific evidence for design, fine tuning, and even the origin of the universe, it is clear to see just how a cumulative and persuasive case for the reality of God is built up.

So, to summarise, our distinctive human nature lies in our capacities to reason, to choose, to be creative, and even to worship. By contrast, in the animal, wrote Emil Brunner:

... we do not see even the smallest beginning of a tendency to seek truth for truth's sake, to shape beauty for the sake of beauty, to promote righteousness for the

sake of righteousness, to reverence the Holy for the sake of its holiness. The animal knows above its immediate sphere of existence, nothing but which it measures or tests its existence. The difference between man and beast amounts to a whole dimension of existence.[69]

Chapter 5

Science and Theism

The fact that an opinion has been
widely held is no evidence that it is not
utterly absurd; indeed, in view of the
silliness of the majority of mankind, a
widespread belief is more likely to be
foolish than sensible.[70]

Bertrand Russell (1872-1970)
British philosopher and mathematician

There is a tendency in our society to accept that the advance
of science has made belief in God untenable. The idea that,
if you understand how things work, there is no need for
any designer to be involved has become popular. Such an
idea flagrantly breaks the rules of logical thought. It is a
bit like saying that because we have unravelled the detailed
complexity of some piece of machinery, it cannot possibly
be designed!

In response to this, Prof John Lennox has argued that you can properly understand a Ford motor car in two ways – in terms of the laws of motion, combustion, and engineering, or by invoking Henry Ford as the genius who originally visualised the construction of motor cars.[71] These are not mutually exclusive explanations. The truth is that complexity, especially when it can be traced to a particular specification, requires a designer.

Peter Atkins, Emeritus Professor of Chemistry at the University of Oxford, however, takes a different view. He is an ardent atheist, and his confidence is based on his understanding of science. Here is a statement of his position:

There is no reason to suppose that science cannot deal with every aspect of existence.[72]

Now, that is clearly not a scientific conclusion but an epistemological proposition; in other words, it's a statement about how we can know what is true. Since it is not a statement that can be scientifically sustained it is self-referentially incoherent. It basically collapses under its own weight.

Prof Richard Dawkins, arguably the best-known atheist of our time, takes a similar view. He finds, for example, that Darwin makes him an intellectually fulfilled atheist.[57] Somehow, by observing small changes in living organisms over time, we have apparently solved the ultimate mystery of how life developed into all the complex biology we find in the living world. For the many good reasons already outlined, we remain to be persuaded!

There is no doubt that the development of science in the West over the last few hundred years is one of the greatest achievements of humankind. With it has come an extensive understanding of the laws and forces that govern the natural world. One of the enduring questions is why modern science arose in the West from around the 16th century and not elsewhere to anything like the same extent.

It is important to note that almost all the great pioneers of Western science were theists, and most were Christians. It is easy to dismiss this by arguing that they were conditioned by the authoritarian nature of the Church and the wider Christian culture of their times. However, Galileo, Copernicus, Kepler, Boyle, Clerk Maxwell, Lord Kelvin, and Sir James Simpson were not the kind of people to bow to peer pressure from churchmen and the like. No, their investigations in the realm of mathematics, physics, astronomy, and chemistry convinced them that they were exploring the handiwork of a supreme intelligence whose works they had begun to uncover.

These giants of science also realised that without the regularity and predictability of the natural world, science would be impossible. They would be astonished at the modern conclusion that our increasing insight into the marvels of the universe should lead us to atheism.

It is not, therefore, too much to claim that it was a theistic view of the universe which gave us modern science in the first place. Here is how Sir Isaac Newton put it:

... Though these bodies may, indeed, persevere in their orbits by the mere laws of gravity, yet they could by no means have, at first, derived the regular position of the orbits themselves from those laws ... this most beautiful system of the sun, planets and comets, could only proceed from the counsel and dominion of an intelligent and powerful Being ... This Being governs all things.[73]

Even Charles Darwin, whose work is so often used to sustain the case for atheism, said:

I have never been an atheist in the sense of denying the existence of a God[39]

... behind all the discernible concatenations, there remains something subtle, intangible and inexplicable. Veneration for this force is my religion. To that extent, I am in point of fact, religious.[78]

Albert Einstein (1879-1955)
German theoretical physicist

It would, however, be wrong to think that it was only the pioneering scientists who were theists. Many of today's practising scientists are Christians, among them Prof John Polkinghorne, former Professor of Theoretical Physics at Cambridge, and Dr Francis Collins, the Director of the Human Genome Project and The National Institutes of Health, who describing his journey to faith wrote:

I began to appreciate that there were pointers to God's existence in the study of nature,[74]

and of the Human Genome project:

For me the experiencing of sequencing the human genome, and uncovering this most remarkable of all texts, was both a stunning scientific achievement and an occasion of worship.[50]

In this connection, it is striking that at an historic trans-Atlantic Press Conference on 26th June 2000 to announce the completion of the Human Genome Project and featuring American President Bill Clinton and British Prime Minister Tony Blair, the statement read by the President said,

Today we are learning the language in which God created life.[75]

Perhaps Francis Collins wrote the script!

It is interesting to note that two decades earlier, Sir Fred Hoyle made this comment about biomaterials:

*If one proceeds directly and straightforwardly in this matter, without being deflected by a fear of incurring the wrath of scientific opinion, one arrives at the conclusion that biomaterials with their amazing measure of order must be the outcome of **intelligent design**. No other possibility I have been able to think of ...*[76, 77] (authors' emphasis)

Assessing Worldviews

So how do the underlying worldviews connect, if at all? There are a couple of ways of looking at this interface. For example, there is the idea that science concerns the natural world and religion deals in the supernatural, so the two disciplines just do not mix, indeed some might say that they are in conflict. Science is concerned with how things work, whereas religion is more focused on 'Why?' rather than 'How?'

It was the Harvard palaeontologist and evolutionary biologist Stephen Jay Gould (1941-2002) who labelled this idea 'non-overlapping magisteria'; that is, that there is really no significant connection between the realms of science and religion, in that they represent totally different areas of investigation and inquiry.

The difficulty, however, is that religion makes scientific claims – claims about existence and origins, and there is no doubt that these are claims that can be legitimately investigated by scientific tools and reasoning. So perhaps the relationship between science and religion is rather more nuanced.

When scientific disciplines and religious inquiry address the same issues, there are often areas of agreement. Examples might include the understanding that the universe had a beginning, or that it demonstrates overwhelming evidence of design, thus implying a designing agency. Some of those of a naturalistic persuasion like philosopher Daniel Dennett (1942-) have an inflated notion of their own intellectual significance. He wrote, 'a Bright is a person with a naturalist as opposed to a supernaturalist world view. We Brights don't believe in ghosts or elves or the Easter Bunny – or God'.[79] The naturalist, inevitably atheistic in outlook, has to propose that the apparent design in the cosmos and in nature is accidental and not real. These questions are open to scientific investigation and so the distinction between science and religion is not clear-cut.

Naturalism and Theism

On closer inspection, and perhaps surprisingly, there is a powerful logical argument showing that conventional science and theism are much more aligned than science and naturalism. This discussion was laid out in detail by the analytical philosopher and logician, Alvin Plantinga (1932-).

He emphasised that when one compares the two worldview positions, naturalism and theism, there are deep-seated differences. Naturalism is a firmly atheistic position; the over-riding idea is that *only* natural and material things exist. Theism, on the other hand, holds that God is real and, to a greater or lesser extent, is active and involved in the operation of the universe.

Most people simply assume that science is much more allied to naturalism than to theism and in fact perceive a conflict between theism and science. Plantinga, however, has argued that, in fact, science conflicts with naturalism and supports theism.[80] So, how does he arrive at such a counter-intuitive conclusion?

It is sometimes suggested that the theory of evolution disproves the existence of God. Many of the supporters of the so-called neo-Darwinian synthesis are atheists. Indeed, if someone is an atheist by conviction, they have no option but to hold to some kind of naturalistic evolutionary story in the form of descent with modification to explain the existence and diversity of life. That, according to Plantinga, is where the problem lies.

The driving force for the evolutionary narrative is believed to be natural selection that filters genetic modifications to preferentially allow the changes that provide a better fit for survival and reproduction to the modified organism. Plantinga's claim is that it is not possible, sensibly, to believe these two things – naturalism and evolution – together. It is natural to assume that our cognitive faculties are basically reliable – that our beliefs are much more likely to be true than false. His argument pivots on an understanding of the reliability of a person's cognitive faculties, intuition, logical reasoning, or ability to remember things.

If naturalism is correct and the evolutionary drive selects for behaviours and characteristics better suited to the environment, it is clear that an individual's behaviour is dependent upon their neurological system which in turn – if evolution is true – has been adapted by natural selection. It is obvious, therefore, that the behaviour emanating from that neural system is also adaptive. It is what helps the individual to survive and to reproduce. The adapted neurological system that causes behaviour is also responsible for a person's belief. However, providing the neurology produces the appropriate adaptive behaviour, the nature and content of their beliefs is irrelevant. They may be true or false – it has no direct bearing on survival. Providing the neurology causes the right kind of adaptive behaviour, the *nature* of their beliefs makes no difference. Certainly, the *truth* of their beliefs makes no difference. Any given belief is as likely to be true as it is to be false – the probability that all their beliefs turn out to be true is very low.

You can probably now sense the problem. If we remain wedded to naturalism and evolution, there is no reason that our cognitive faculties can be considered to be reliable; that is, that amongst the many things we may believe, there is a preponderance of true beliefs over false beliefs.

So, hold on a second. Surely it would be the case that our beliefs would be more likely to be true than false if the neurology is adaptive? Well not exactly. Providing the behaviour and underlying neurology are adaptive – it makes no difference to natural selection whether the beliefs are true or false. Natural selection is interested in behaviour, so the nature, content, and veracity of our beliefs are irrelevant.

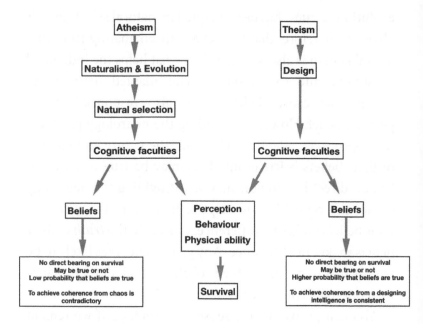

This then is the issue. If, given naturalism and evolution, the probability of our cognitive faculties being reliable is low, this challenges our instinctive assumption that our beliefs are correct. Our cognitive faculties including our beliefs are unreliable. In fact, this is a huge problem for any and all beliefs we might hold if naturalism and evolution are true. A person's belief system becomes self-referentially incoherent! If someone is a naturalist they will inevitably have to hold to some kind of adaptive evolutionary view and any beliefs they hold on that basis could be right or wrong, but they certainly cannot hold them with confidence that their cognitive faculties and understanding are reliable. At best they would really have to hold all their beliefs with a healthy measure of skepticism.

It is also worth pointing out that this reasoning is not an argument against naturalism or indeed an argument against evolution. It is, however, an argument concluding that one cannot sensibly hold to both naturalism and evolution together – they are in deep and irreconcilable conflict.

If, in contrast, one makes an appeal to theism, it quickly becomes apparent that an appeal to theistic design, rather than the blind forces of nature can more readily explain why we can be confident in our reasoning and secure in the beliefs that result from our cognitive faculties.

In summary, science, in this instance, is in serious and perhaps irreparable conflict with naturalism. Combining evolutionary theory with naturalism leads to the conclusion that there is almost nothing we can really know, with any degree of confidence, about ourselves or about our world.

So, if we follow the science, in which direction does it take us? To naturalism or to design? To atheism, or to theism? We hope we have persuaded you that the answer is clear – the evidence points to a transcendent, powerful designer!

Authors' Postscript

> Overwhelming strong proofs
> of intelligent and benevolent
> design lie around us ... The atheistic
> idea is so nonsensical that I cannot put
> it into words.[81]
>
> Lord Kelvin (1824-1907)
> British physicist and engineer

We are both Christians and have professional backgrounds in medicine, science, and education. The impetus for writing this book was a growing astonishment on our part that the scientific community has almost entirely adopted a position, not just of methodological naturalism, but ideological naturalism which implies atheism. We hope we present a counterbalance to the prevalent view that science has rendered faith and, in particular, belief in a creator outdated and contradicted by the scientific facts. We hold that nothing could be further from the truth and hope that this volume explains our reasons for that position.

It is often forgotten that Western science has developed from a basis of Christian theism, which held that it was the order and predictability of the universe which made rational investigation possible. More recent discoveries in molecular biology, together with the enduring mystery of mind and consciousness, point overwhelmingly to intelligent design in nature. We argue, therefore that, at the very least, the design argument should be an area of legitimate debate in science and not dismissed as 'pseudo-science'.

However, we recognise that Christian faith is not ultimately based on scientific arguments or philosophical presuppositions, but is rooted in historical realities, and in particular the crucifixion and resurrection of Jesus Christ. From these indisputable facts flow the theological implications of sin, forgiveness, faith, and personal fulfilment.

A significant number of scientists would concur with these sentiments. One example from the 19th century was Sir James Young Simpson (1811-1870), the medical scientist who helped to pioneer the use of anaesthesia and was the first to demonstrate the value of chloroform in treating patients.[82] Ether was an alternative agent, already gaining ground in Boston following some demonstrations in the Bullfinch Building at the Massachusetts General Hospital.

Simpson was reputed to be Queen Victoria's favourite doctor and he became famous for using chloroform as an anaesthetic agent. In fact, he self-administered this strong smelling trichloromethane in an experiment conducted in his own dining room! He was fortunate not to have inhaled a fatal overdose! Moving from these trials, he ventured to use chloroform clinically in the late 1840s and even used it on the Queen when she was in labour with her son, Leopold, the eighth child and youngest son of Queen Victoria and Prince Albert. The result was a significant increase in public confidence and these wonder drugs gained enormous levels of acceptability. Simpson was a committed Christian and a devout member and elder of the St Columba's Free Church of Scotland. He also set up the Medical Dispensary for the poor in Carrubbers Close Mission on the Royal Mile.

Once a journalist asked him what his greatest discovery was. He replied clearly:

That I am a sinner, and that Jesus is a great Saviour!

Simpson also wrote in his personal testimony:

But again, I looked and saw JESUS, my substitute, scourged in my stead and dying on the cross for me. I looked and cried and was forgiven. And it seems to be my duty to tell you of that Saviour, to see if you will not also look and live: How simple it all becomes when the Holy Spirit opens the eyes! [83]

Sir James Young Simpson clearly did not have a problem with being a leading medical scientist and publicly acknowledging a personal commitment to Christ and the Christian faith. Both then and now, he would not be alone!

The Cavendish Laboratory, Department of Physics, University of Cambridge.

Many significant scientific discoveries were made in the Cavendish. Some 30 researchers later won Nobel Prizes. The first Professor of Physics was the Scottish scientist James Clerk Maxwell (1831-1879) who formulated the classical theory of electromagnetic radiation.

Ernest Rutherford (1871-1937), a nuclear physicist from New Zealand, was also the Professor of Physics here and he differentiated alpha and beta radiation and described the concept of radioactive half-life. The molecular biologists James Watson (b1928) and Francis Crick (1916-2004) worked out the double helical structure of DNA at the Cavendish in February 1953 and published their findings in *Nature* in late April that same year.

Many other remarkable discoveries were made here including the electron, and the neutron.

The inscription placed above the doors of the original Cavendish Laboratory in the University of Cambridge came from a version of the Vulgate – a 4th century Latin translation of the Bible – quoting from the Psalms.

Magna opera Domini exquisita in omnes
voluntates ejus

The English (King James) version of Psalm 111:2 was placed over the doors of the laboratory's new building in 1974.

The works of the Lord are great,
sought out of all them that have
pleasure therein

INDEX

Abduction, 48, 50

Abiogenesis, 65-70, 78

Adaptation, 81-83

Atkins, Peter, 110

Behe Michael J., 80, 95-96, 99, 103

Bertalanffy, Ludwig von, 84

Birney, Ewan, 89

Bryson, Bill, 60

Cairns-Smith, Alexander Graham, 75

Cavendish Laboratory, 124-125

Chirality, 73-75

Collins, Francis, 87, 113

Common descent, 81, 83, 86

COVID-19, 24, 29, 32, 45-46

Cox, Brian, 58

Coyne, Jerry, 80

Craig, William Lane, 57

Crick, Francis, 100, 124

Darwin, Charles, 54, 71-72, 79, 81-87, 89-92, 110, 112

Davies, Paul, 58, 92

Dawkins, Richard, 80, 89, 110

Deduction, 48-49

Dennett, Daniel, 115

Denton, Michael, 102

DNA, deoxyribonucleic acid, 67, 76, 80-83, 87-89, 99-102

Economist, 41

Eddington, Sir Arthur, 53, 55

Einstein, Albert, 55, 63, 112

Eiseley, Loren, 52

Eldredge, Niles, 91

ENCODE, 87-88

Falsifiability, 43

Fine tuning, 60-64

Fisher, Ronald, 42

Flagellum, bacterial, 95-97

Fossil Record, 79, 89-91

Fuller, Prof Steve, 92-93

Gates, Bill, 101

Gitt, Werner, 102

Gould, Stephen Jay, 48, 90, 114

Haeckel, Ernst, 71

Hawking, Stephen, 60

Hodgson, Peter, 104-105

Hoyle, Sir Fred, 56, 61, 113

Hubble, Edwin, 55

Hydrothermal vents, 76

Iceland, 31

Induction, 48-49

Information, 83-84, 89, 100-102

Intelligent design, 92-93, 114-115, 121

Irreducible Complexity, 95-98

Jastrow, Robert, 57

Job, 138

Junk DNA, 87, 89

Kalam cosmological argument, 49

Kelvin, Lord (William Thomson), 111, 121

Lennox, John, 110

Lenski, Richard, 98-99

Lewontin, Richard, 35, 57

Lyell, Charles, 71-72

Materialism, 35, 65, 86

Meyer, Stephen C., 84, 104

Milky Way, 54

Miller – Urey experiment, 66-67

Miller, Stanley, 67

Mind and Consciousness, 28, 33, 36, 103-105

Molecular Machines, 72, 77, 80, 95

Morality and Conscience, 105

Multiverse, 62

Nagel, Thomas, 37, 104

Needham, John, 70

Newton, Sir Isaac, 58, 63, 111-112

Nutt, David, 46

Oken, Lorenz, 69

Origin of Life Research, 72-78

Paine, Thomas, 25

Pasteur, Louis, 70-71, 74

Peer Review, 42-43

Plantinga, Alvin, 115-116

Polkinghorne, John, 113

Popper, Karl, 43

Raup, David M., 91

Redi, Francesco, 69

RNA world, 76-77

Royal Society, 86

Russell, Bertrand, 109

Sagan, Carl, 53

SARS-CoV-2, 21, 29

Schleiden, Matthias, 69

Scientific Method, 28, 39-41

Scientism, 52

Second Law of Thermodynamics, 56

Shapiro, James, 85-86

Simpson, Sir James Young, 111, 122

South Korea, 31

Spallanzani, Lazzaro, 70

Steady State Model, 56

Sub-set analysis, 45

Today Programme, 45, 47

Tour, James, 78

Updike, John, 54

Urey, Harold, 66-67

Walport, Sir Mark, 45

Watson, James D., 100, 124

Winston, Lord Robert, 47

Wuhan, 29

Yockey, Hubert P., 65

GLOSSARY

A priori – requiring no evidence for validation or support.

Abduction – arriving at a conclusion by inference when direct evidence is not available.

Abiogenesis – the hypothetical process by which living organisms are thought to arise from inanimate matter.

Biodiversity – the wide range of living organisms on the planet.

Biosphere – the part of the earth's surface and atmosphere inhabited by living things.

Cherry-picking – the suppression evidence by pointing to individual cases or data sets that seem to confirm a particular position whilst ignoring a significant portion of related and similar cases or data that may produce an alternative conclusion.

Chirality – the configuration or handedness (left or right) of an asymmetrical chemical molecule.

Chloroform – another name for trichloromethane – a sweet-smelling liquid used as a solvent and formerly as an anaesthetic.

Cilia – any of the short dynamic threads or hairs projecting from a cell that serve to move fluid over the cell surface.

Coronavirus – a virus with a distinctive circular or crown-like shape.

Cosmology – the study of the origin and the nature of the universe.

Deduction – the process of reasoning in which the conclusion follows logically from the premises.

Dextro-rotatory – the property of right-handedness in asymmetrical molecules.

DNA – deoxyribonucleic acid is the main constituent of the chromosomes of all organisms. Its molecular structure is in the form of a double helix and the order of the chemical units along its length carries the genetic information which builds the organism and all its constituent parts. It is a massively complex information processing system.

Dynein – a family of motor proteins that move along microtubules in cells.

E.coli – Escherichia coli; a type of bacteria common in human and animal intestines, and forms part of the normal gut flora.

Electromagnetic – refers to a branch of physics involving the study of the electromagnetic force, a type of physical interaction that occurs between electrically charged particles. A magnetic field is associated with the flow of electrons to provide an electric current.

ENCODE – the project based at Cambridge to investigate the existence and function of the coded areas of D NA.

Endocrine – The endocrine system is a series of glands that produce and secrete hormones that the body uses for a wide range of functions.

Entropy – a measure of the disorder of a closed system.

Epigenetic – the epigenome consists of chemical compounds that modify or mark the genome in such a way that the instructions in the DNA code can be modified by external factors.

Evolution – gradual change in the characteristics of animals and plants over time.

Falsifiability – the contradiction of a hypothesis by credible evidence to the contrary.

Fine tuning – the process in which parameters of a model must be adjusted very precisely in order to fit with certain observations.

Flagellum – a tail-like outgrowth from a cell which acts as an organ of locomotion.

Gene – the basic physical and functional unit of heredity.

Genetic – relating to genes and the source of inherited characteristics.

Homochiral – the property of asymmetrical molecules that possess the same configuration or handedness.

Hydrogen bonds – weak chemical bonds between molecules involving atoms of nitrogen, fluorine or oxygen atoms in one molecule, and a hydrogen atom in another.

Hypothesis – a proposed explanation made on the basis of limited evidence as a starting point for further investigation.

Induction – inductive reasoning makes broad generalisations from specific observations allowing conclusions to be drawn from data.

Inorganic – with reference to all the chemical elements apart from carbon and carbon-based compounds.

Isomer – molecules that have the same molecular formula, but have a different arrangement of the atoms in space.

Intelligent design – intelligent design theory holds that certain features of the universe and of living things are best explained by an intelligent cause.

Irreducible complexity – describes a system in which multiple parts are arranged to yield function. If any components are removed or damaged the function is degraded or lost.

Junk DNA – regions of non-coding DNA formerly thought to be devoid of function.

Kinesin – motor protein that moves along intracellular microtubules like dyneins. Kinesin moves in the opposite direction to dynein relative to the configuration of the microtubule.

Krebs cycle – A series of chemical reactions that occur in most aerobic organisms and are part of the process of carbohydrate metabolism, by which glucose and other molecules are broken down in the presence of oxygen into carbon dioxide and water to release chemical energy in the form of ATP.

Levorotatory – the property of left-handedness in asymmetrical molecules.

Materialism – the theory that nothing exists except matter and energy.

Mutation – a change in the sequence of nucleotide bases in DNA.

Myosin – a motor protein involved in the process of muscle contraction.

Natural selection – the process through which populations of living organisms adapt and change thus filtering and preserving those better suited to environmental conditions.

Naturalism – the idea that everything in the universe including laws and forces are natural as distinct from supernatural.

Neo-Darwinian – descriptive of the modern version of Darwin's theory of evolution by natural selection, incorporating the findings of genetics that were unknown to Darwin in the 19th century.

Nuclear physics – study of the subatomic particles and their interactions.

Organic – organic chemistry is the study of the structure, properties, composition, reactions, and preparation of carbon-containing compounds.

Peer review – the independent evaluation of work by those with similar competencies to the producers of the work.

Pharmacology – study of the mechanisms of action of drugs.

Polymer – very large molecule composed of many repeating subunits.

Protein – large molecules composed of one or more long chains of amino acids. Some are structural, others functional e.g. antibodies and enzymes.

Pseudogene – nonfunctional segments of DNA that resemble functional genes.

Racemic – a term used to describe a mixture of left and right handed forms of a chemical compound in equal proportion.

Red-shift – stretching of the wavelength of light such that it is 'shifted' towards the red end of the electromagnetic spectrum.

Reductionism – the practice of analysing and describing a complex phenomenon in terms of its simple or fundamental constituents.

Relativity – two inter-related theories of relativity described by Albert Einstein: special relativity (published in 1905) and general relativity (published in 1915).

Reliability – in experimental science it is the degree of reproducibility of results expressed as a percentage.

Replication – the process of duplicating or producing an exact copy.

RNA – A nucleic acid similar to DNA although the chemical structure is configured differently: the sugar phosphate chain contains ribose rather than deoxyribose and the pyrimidine base uracil rather than thymine.

Scientism – the view that science provides the only way of knowing the objective truth about reality.

Specified complexity – a pattern or arrangement that displays a large amount of independently specified information with a low probability of chance occurrence.

Spontaneous generation – the hypothetical process by which living organisms develop from non-living matter.

Sub-set analysis – A form of cherry picking where e.g. in a clinical study, the evaluation of results is restricted to only some of the patients who participated.

Syllogism – A way of expressing a logical argument such that a conclusion can be drawn from two given or assumed premises.

Thermodynamics – the branch of physics that deals with the relationships between different forms of energy.

Trichloromethane – see chloroform.

Van der Waals forces – forces of attraction or repulsion between atoms and molecules caused by fluctuating polarisation of the particles.

Worldview – a framework of ideas and beliefs providing an overall appreciation by which a person understands, interprets and interacts with the world.

> Where were you when I laid the earth's foundation? Tell me, if you understand. Who marked off its dimensions? Surely you know! Who stretched a measuring line across it? On what were its footings set, or who laid its cornerstone?
>
> Book of Job 38:4-6
> Bible (New International Version)

References

1. Only child benefits – show me the research! [Internet]. ResearchAddict. 2018 [cited 2020 Nov 20]. Available from: https://researchaddict.com/only-child-benefits-research/

2. Dedication < Thomas Paine – The age of Reason (1794) American History From Revolution To Reconstruction and beyond [Internet]. [cited 2020 Nov 6]. Available from: http://www.let.rug.nl/usa/documents/1786-1800/thomas-paine-the-age-of-reason/dedication.php

3. WHO Coronavirus Disease (COVID-19) Dashboard [Internet]. [cited 2021 Jan 25]. Available from: https://covid19.who.int

4. Leavitt MO. Words of Wisdom [Internet]. Quoted in Telliamed Revisited. 2020 [cited 2020 Nov 6]. Available from: https://telliamedrevisited.wordpress.com/2020/02/29/words-of-wisdom/

5. Park YJ, Choe YJ, Park O, Park SY, Kim Y-M, Kim J, et al. Contact Tracing during Coronavirus Disease Outbreak, South Korea, 2020. Emerging Infectious Diseases Journal – CDC;2020:26:10. [cited 2020

Sep 28]; Available from: https://wwwnc.cdc.gov/eid/article/26/10/20-1315_article

6. Coronavirus: Hunting down COVID-19 [Internet]. Science Museum Group. [cited 2020 Sep 28]. Available from: https://www.sciencemuseumgroup.org.uk/blog/hunting-down-covid-19

7. Lewontin, Richard C. Billions and Billions of Demons. 1997 Jan 9 [cited 2019 Mar 5]; Available from: https://www.nybooks.com/articles/1997/01/09/billions-and-billions-of-demons/

8. Nagel T. Public Education and Intelligent Design. Philosophy and Public Affairs. 2008 36(2):187–205.

9. Campbell NA, Reece JB, Mitchell LG. Biology. 5th Edition. Benjamin Cummings; 1999.

10. Trouble at the lab. The Economist [Internet]. 2013 Oct 18 [cited 2020 Sep 28]; Available from: https://www.economist.com/briefing/2013/10/18/trouble-at-the-lab

11. Allison DB, Brown AW, George BJ, Kaiser KA. Reproducibility: A tragedy of errors. Nature News. 2016 Feb 4;530(7588):27.

12. Godlee F, Gale CR, Martyn CN. Effect on the Quality of Peer Review of Blinding Reviewers and Asking Them to Sign Their Reports: A Randomized Controlled Trial. JAMA. 1998 280(3):237–40.

13. Eiseley L, Hothaus G. The Firmament of Time. Bison

Books; 1999.

14. Smith GD, Blastland M, Munafò M. Covid-19's known unknowns. BMJ [Internet]. 2020 Oct 19 [cited 2020 Nov 21];371. Available from: https://www.bmj.com/content/371/bmj.m3979

15. Nutt D, King LA, Saulsbury W, Blakemore C. Development of a rational scale to assess the harm of drugs of potential misuse. The Lancet. 2007 369(9566):1047–53.

16. Gould SJ. In the Mind of the Beholder. Natural History. 1994 Feb;94(2):14.

17. Craig WL. Reasonable Faith: Christian Truth and Apologetics. Crossway USA; 2008.

18. Sagan C. Cosmos. Random House; 1980.

19. Eddington AS. The End of the World: from the Standpoint of Mathematical Physics. Nature. 1931 127(3203):447–53.

20. Lemaître G. The Beginning of the World from the Point of View of Quantum Theory. Nature. 1931 127(3210):706–706.

21. Ross HW, White KSA, editors. The New Yorker, Volume 85, Issues 1-7. Digitized 30 March 2011. F-R Publishing Corporation;

22. Geisler NL, Turek F. I don't have enough faith to be an atheist. Crossway Books; 2004.

23. Lewontin RC. The Inferiority Complex. [cited 2020 Nov 6]; Available from: https://www.nybooks.com/articles/1981/10/22/the-inferiority-complex/

24. Jastrow R. God And The Astronomers. W. W. Norton & Company; 2001.

25. The Ultimate Question of Origins: God and the Beginning of the Universe | Reasonable Faith [Internet]. [cited 2020 Oct 27]. Available from: http://www.reasonablefaith.org/writings/scholarly-writings/the-existence-of-god/the-ultimate-question-of-origins-god-and-the-beginning-of-the-universe/

26. Davies P. The Goldilocks Enigma. Penguin; 2006.

27. The universe and the Laws [Internet]. Relics World Quotes. 2019 [cited 2020 Oct 27]. Available from: https://www.relicsworld.com/stephen-hawking/the-universe-and-the-laws-of-physics-seem-to-have-been-specifically-author

28. Bryson B. A Short History of Nearly Everything. Black Swan. 2016.

29. Lewis GF, Barnes LA. A Fortunate Universe: Life in a Finely Tuned Cosmos. Cambridge University Press; 2016.

30. Hoyle F. The Universe: Past and Present Reflections. Engineering and Science. 1981 Nov;11:8–12.

31. Vilenkin's Cosmic Vision: A Review Essay of Many Worlds in One: The Search for Other Universes | Reasonable Faith [Internet]. [cited 2020 Nov 24]. Available from: http://www.reasonablefaith.org/writings/scholarly-writings/the-existence-of-god/vilenkins-cosmic-vision-a-review-essay-of-many-worlds-in-one-the-search-for/

32. Yockey H. A Calculation of the Probability of Spontaneous Biogenesis by Information Theory. Journal of Theoretical Biology. 1977;67:398.

33. Fox D. Primordial Soup's On: Scientists Repeat Evolution's Most Famous Experiment [Internet]. Scientific American. [cited 2020 Nov 17]. Available from: https://www.scientificamerican.com/article/primordial-soup-urey-miller-evolution-experiment-repeated/

34. Misslin R. A life of the cell: forms and space. Rev Synth. 2003;(124):205–21.

35. Francesco Redi. In: Wikipedia [Internet]. 2020 [cited 2020 Nov 8]. Available from: https://en.wikipedia.org/w/index.php?title=Francesco_Redi&oldid=979847326

36. Ariatti A, Mandrioli P. Lazzaro spallanzani: A blow against spontaneous generation. Aerobiologia. 1993 Dec 1;9(2):101–7.

37. Wald G. The Origin of Life. Scientific American. 1954 Aug;191(2):46.

38. Ernst Haeckel – Conservapedia [Internet]. [cited 2020 Oct 31]. Available from: https://www.conservapedia.com/Ernst_Haeckel

39. Darwin C. https://www.darwinproject.ac.uk/letter/DCP-LETT-12041.xml [Internet]. Darwin Correspondence Project. [cited 2020 Oct 7]. Available from: https://www.darwinproject.ac.uk/letter/DCP-LETT-12041.xml

40. Sevin A. Pasteur and Molecular Chirality. BibNum. 2015 Apr 15;11.

41. Tour, James. An Open Letter to My Colleagues – James Tour – Inference [Internet]. Inference: International Review of Science. [cited 2019 Mar 5]. Available from: https://inference-review.com/article/an-open-letter-to-my-colleagues

42. Behe MJ. The Edge of Evolution: The Search for the Limits of Darwinism. The Free Press; 2008.

43. Dawkins, Richard. The Greatest Show on Earth: The Evidence for Evolution. Bantam Press; 2010.

44. Coyne JA. Why Evolution is True. OUP Oxford; 1st edition 2010.

45. Behe M. Darwin Devolves: The New Science About DNA That Challenges Evolution. HarperOne; 2019.

46. Meyer SC. Darwin's Doubt: the explosive origin of animal life and the case for intelligent design. First

Edition. New York, NY: HarperOne, an imprint of HarperCollinsPublishers; 2013.

47. Who Was Ludwig von Bertalanffy and Why Does He Matter? [Internet]. Evolution News. 2018 [cited 2020 Nov 20]. Available from: https://evolutionnews.org/2018/07/who-was-ludwig-von-bertalanffy-and-why-does-he-matter/

48. Fodor J, Piatelli-Palmarini, M. What Darwin Got Wrong. Profile Books; 2010.

49. Shapiro JA. Evolution: A View from the 21st Century. Financial Times/ Prentice Hall; 2011.

50. Collins FS. The Language of God A Scientist Presents Evidence for Belief. Simon & Schuster UK; New Ed Edition; 2007.

51. The ENCODE Project Consortium. An integrated encyclopedia of DNA elements in the human genome. Nature. 2012 Sep 6;489:57–74.

52. ENCODE: Encyclopedia Of DNA Elements [Internet]. 2012 [cited 2020 Nov 9]. Available from: https://www.youtube.com/watch?v=Y3V2thsJ1Wc&feature=youtu.be

53. Huxley Memorial Debate 1986 02 14 (4 Dr Richard Dawkins – New College) [Internet]. 2014 [cited 2020 Nov 1]. Available from: https://www.youtube.com/watch?v=j-q-ht5csYY

54. Gould SJ. Is a new and general theory of evolution emerging? Paleobiology. 1980;6(1):119–30.

55. Eldredge N, Tattersall I. The Myths of Human Evolution. New York: Columbia Universty Press; Reprint edition; 1984.

56. David Raup – RationalWiki [Internet]. [cited 2020 Nov 1]. Available from: https://rationalwiki.org/wiki/David_Raup

57. Dawkins, Richard. The Blind Watchmaker. W.W. Norton & Company, Inc; 1996.

58. Moreland JP, editor. Theistic evolution: a scientific, philosophical, and theological critique. Crossway; 2017.

59. Hoyle F. Intelligent Universe: A New View of Creation and Evolution. Michael Joseph Ltd; 1983.

60. Behe MJ. Darwin's Black Box: The Biochemical Challenge to Evolution. Free Press; 2 Rev Ed edition; 2006.

61. Liu R, Ochman H. Stepwise formation of the bacterial flagellar system. PNAS. 2007 Apr 24;104(17):7116–21.

62. Gates B, Myhrvold N, Rinearson P. The Road Ahead. Viking; 1995.

63. Gitt W. In the Beginning Was Information: A Scientist Explains the Incredible Design in Nature. New Leaf Publishing; 2006.

64. Denton M. Evolution: A Theory in Crisis. Adler & Adler Publishers Inc.,U.S; 1996.

65. Nagel, Thomas. Mind and Cosmos: Why the Materialist Neo-Darwinian Conception of Nature Is Almost Certainly False. Oxford, New York: Oxford University Press; 2012.

66. Meyer SC. Signature in the cell: DNA and the evidence for intelligent design. 1st ed. New York: HarperOne; 2009.

67. Burkart JM, Brügger RK, van Schaik CP. Evolutionary Origins of Morality: Insights From Non-human Primates. Front Sociol [Internet]. 2018 [cited 2020 Oct 31];3. Available from: https://www.frontiersin.org/articles/10.3389/fsoc.2018.00017/full

68. Singer P. Ethics | Origins, History, Theories, & Applications [Internet]. Encyclopedia Britannica. [cited 2020 Oct 31]. Available from: https://www.britannica.com/topic/ethics-philosophy

69. Brunner E. Man in Revolt. Westminster John Knox; 1979.

70. Russell, Bertrand. Marriage and Morals. Routledge; 1985.

71. Lennox JC. God's Undertaker: Has Science Buried God? Lion Books; 2009.

72. Cornwell, John, editor. The Limitless Power of Science. In: Nature's Imagination – The Frontiers of Scientific Vision. Oxford: Oxford university Press; 1995.

73. Newton I. 'General Scholium' from the Mathematical Principles of Natural Philosophy (1729) (Normalized) [Internet]. The Newton Project. 2009 [cited 2020 Oct

7]. Available from: http://www.newtonproject.ox.ac.uk/view/texts/normalized/NATP00056

74. Berry RJ, editor. Real Scientists Real Faith: 17 Leading Scientists Reveal the Harmony Between Their Science and Their Faith. Monarch Books; 2009.

75. President Clinton: Announcing The Completion Of The First Survey Of The Entire Human Genome June 26, 2000 [Internet]. [cited 2020 Oct 7]. Available from: https://clintonwhitehouse3.archives.gov/WH/Work/062600.html

76. Hoyle F. Evolution from Space. Omni Lecture, Royal Institution; 1982 Jan 12; London.

77. Hoyle F, Wickramasinghe C. Evolution from Space. Simon & Schuster; 1984.

78. Kessler H. The Diaries Of A Cosmopolitan 1918-1937. Weidenfeld & Nicolson; 1999.

79. Dennett DC. Opinion | The Bright Stuff (Published 2003). The New York Times [Internet]. 2003 Jul 12 [cited 2020 Oct 9]; Available from: https://www.nytimes.com/2003/07/12/opinion/the-bright-stuff.html

80. Plantinga A. Where the Conflict Really Lies: Science, Religion, and Naturalism. OUP USA; 2012.

81. Winston R. Improving on humanity. Nature. 2002 Apr 25;416:792–3.

82. James Young Simpson. In: Wikipedia [Internet].
2020 [cited 2020 Nov 6]. Available from: https://
en.wikipedia.org/w/index.php?title=James_Young_
Simpson&oldid=987091431

83. James-Griffiths P. Sir James Young Simpson (1811-
1870) [Internet]. Christian Heritage Edinburgh. 2016
[cited 2020 Nov 20]. Available from: https://www.
christianheritageedinburgh.org.uk/2016/08/23/sir-
james-young-simpson-1811-1870/

Image credits

p74. Amino acid chirality – From https://en.wikipedia.org/ wiki/Chirality#/media/File:Chirality_with_hands.svg Public Domain, https://commons. wikimedia.org/w/index.php?curid=17071045

p96. Used with permission Timothy G. Standish, PhD, Senior Scientist, Geoscience Research Institute, Loma Linda, CA 92350

p97 https://www.shutterstock.com/image-illustration/3drenderedillustration-motor-protein-1215278065

p101 Used with permission Timothy G. Standish, PhD, Senior Scientist, Geoscience Research Institute, Loma Linda, CA 92350

p118 David Galloway and Alastair Noble 2021

OTHER BOOKS BY THESE AUTHORS

Alastair Noble:

And Is It True? (with Dr Stephen McQuoid), Authentic Media, 2004.

An Introduction to Intelligent Design, Centre for Intelligent Design, 2013.

Born in a Golden Age, John Ritchie Publishing, 2019.

David Galloway:

Controlled Chaos. Surgical Adventures in Chitokoloki Mission Hospital, (with Dr Jenni Galloway), John Ritchie Publishing, 2020.

Design Dissected. Is the Design Real? John Ritchie Publishing, 2021.